T0139653

THE AGE OF ALGORITHMS

Algorithms are probably the most sophisticated tools that men have had
at their disposal since the beginnings of human history. They have
transformed science, industry, and society. They upset the concepts of
work, property, government, private life, even humanity. Going easily from
one extreme to the other, we rejoice that they make life easier for us, but
fear that they will enslave us. To get beyond this vision of good vs. evil,
this book takes a new look at our time, the Age of Algorithms. Creations
of the human spirit, algorithms are what we made them. And they
will be what we want them to be: it is up to us to choose the world we want
to live in.

Serge Abiteboul is a member of the Board of Arcep and a computer
scientist at Inria. He has been visiting professor at Stanford University
and is a founder of the Xyleme company. He is fascinated by and likes
to write about societal issues related to the digital world.

Gilles Dowek is a researcher in computer science. He has published
several popular science books and books on epistemology of computer
science and ethics in the digital world. His book *Computation,
Proof, Machine* (Cambridge University Press) has received the
French Academy philosophy award.

THE AGE
OF
ALGORITHMS

Serge
ABITEBOUL

Gilles
DOWEK

CAMBRIDGE
UNIVERSITY PRESS

CAMBRIDGE
UNIVERSITY PRESS

University Printing House, Cambridge CB2 8BS, United Kingdom

One Liberty Plaza, 20th Floor, New York, NY 10006, USA

477 Williamstown Road, Port Melbourne, VIC 3207, Australia

314–321, 3rd Floor, Plot 3, Splendor Forum, Jasola District Centre,
New Delhi – 110025, India

79 Anson Road, #06–04/06, Singapore 079906

Cambridge University Press is part of the University of Cambridge.

It furthers the University's mission by disseminating knowledge in the pursuit of
education, learning, and research at the highest international levels of excellence.

www.cambridge.org
Information on this title: www.cambridge.org/9781108484572
DOI: 10.1017/9781108614139

© Cambridge University Press 2020

This publication is in copyright. Subject to statutory exception
and to the provisions of relevant collective licensing agreements,
no reproduction of any part may take place without the written
permission of Cambridge University Press.

First published as *Le temps des algorithmes* by Editions Le Pommier 2020

English translation 2020

Printed in the United States of America by Sheridan Books, Inc.

A catalogue record for this publication is available from the British Library.

Library of Congress Cataloging-in-Publication Data
Names: Abiteboul, S. (Serge), author. | Dowek, Gilles, author.
Title: The age of algorithms / Serge Abiteboul, Aachen University of Technology,
Gilles Dowek, Ecole Normale Supérieure, Saclay.
Description: Cambridge, United Kingdom ; New York, NY : Cambridge
University Press, 2018.
Identifiers: LCCN 2019044718 (print) | LCCN 2019044719 (ebook) |
ISBN 9781108484572 (hardback) | ISBN 9781108745420 (paperback) |
ISBN 9781108614139 (epub)
Subjects: LCSH: Algorithms.
Classification: LCC QA9.58 .A245 2018 (print) | LCC QA9.58 (ebook) |
DDC 518/.1–dc23
LC record available at https://lccn.loc.gov/2019044718
LC ebook record available at https://lccn.loc.gov/2019044719

ISBN 978-1-108-48457-2 Hardback
ISBN 978-1-108-74542-0 Paperback

Cambridge University Press has no responsibility for the persistence or accuracy
of URLs for external or third-party internet websites referred to in this publication
and does not guarantee that any content on such websites is, or will remain,
accurate or appropriate.

CONTENTS

ACKNOWLEDGMENTS

We wish to thank Bertrand Braunschweig, Laurent Fribourg, Sophie Gamerman, Florence Hachez-Leroy, Marie Jung, Xavier de La Porte, Michel Puech, and Michel Volle for their pertinent comments on an early version of this text.

We would also like to thank Jean-Pierre Archambault, Gérard Berry, Maurice Nivat, and many others for the often passionate discussions on the topics addressed in this book.

1

Algorithms Intrigue, Algorithms Disturb

Algorithms have become an essential component of our professional lives and social interactions, in health care, transportation, commerce, industry. Algorithms are transforming the natural sciences, social sciences, and the humanities, and in doing so, enrich our knowledge. They allow technology to continually push beyond the limits of the possible.

Some algorithms, such as telephone operating systems, data management systems, or search engines, are huge things involving the contributions of thousands of people. They are sometimes compared to cathedrals, in that they share the same ambition, and the same folly.

With algorithms, it appears that *Homo sapiens* have finally created a tool equal to their aspirations.

However, there is also a worrisome side to these algorithms. The profession of mail carrier is disappearing? Algorithms are destroying jobs. An insurance company compensates the victim of an accident? A cynical algorithm computes the amount of the compensation. The stock market takes a dive? Trading algorithms are responsible for the crash. Laws restrict civil liberties? Government algorithms are spying on us. Algorithms beat humans at chess and at Go? Intelligent algorithms will soon govern us.

Why do we blame algorithms for our woes? Because they push us out of our comfort zone? Without a doubt. But also because we often agree to use them, not understanding what they really are and how they work. Our dreams and our fears are the consequences of this ignorance. We fear algorithms because we see them as mysterious beings, endowed with supernatural powers, even evil intentions.

To free ourselves from this magical thinking, to separate legitimate hopes from childish fantasies, justified fears from unfounded anxieties, we invite the reader on a journey through the world of algorithms during the course of which we will encounter some of the challenges facing us in the age of algorithms: the transformation of work, the disappearance of property, and the protection of privacy, to name a few.

Algorithms can lead to the best or the worst outcome, but we must never forget that they do not, in themselves, have intention. They have been designed by human beings. They are what we want them to be.

— *Hello, Robot. Tell me what an algorithm is.*
— *OK, but I'll also need to talk about the relationship between algorithms, computers, and programs.*
— *I know. When we have found an algorithm, we write it in the form of a program and then we just ask a computer to work for us.*
— *Exactly.*
— *So everything is possible with algorithms?*
— *No. But that may be what makes them even more intriguing.*

2

What Is an Algorithm?

In order to understand what an algorithm is, let's begin by taking a trip back a few millennia in the past to imagine one of our distant ancestors who had seen his late grandmother bake bread and then tries it himself. He doesn't really know what to do. He hesitates, starts by boiling grains of wheat in water, then realizes it might be a bad idea. He does what we all do when confronted with a problem that we don't know how to resolve: we think of solutions, we try them out, we feel our way, counting on a touch of serendipity until we succeed, or not.

Real bakers, however, don't work like this. They don't reinvent the bread recipe each time, because they have learned how to make it and they remember how to do it. And because they have this recipe, they can give us our daily bread. Indeed, civilization develops because people invent things, but also because others copy these inventions and sometimes improve on them.

We have forgotten just how valuable the bread recipe is. First of all, it helps reduce uncertainty: with the recipe, the baker knows that unless there is a catastrophe, the bread will be ready for dinner. This recipe requires neither imagination nor talent. The authors of this book, for example, having no talent at all for bread baking, can find a chapati recipe online and make some perfectly reasonable flatbreads, following in the footsteps of more imaginative and talented bakers than themselves.

This recipe is part of our heritage: it has been passed from generation to generation for millennia.

This recipe is an algorithm and it provides us with an initial definition of the concept. An algorithm is a procedure that allows us to solve a problem without having to invent a solution each time.

With this definition, it is clear that since the dawn of humanity, we have been inventing, using, and passing on algorithms for activities such as cooking, flint knapping, fishing, and growing lentils and wheat.

Procedures and Symbols

Unlike the bread recipe, certain algorithms can solve problems dealing with written symbols, such as numbers and letters, that are combined to form numbers, words, sentences, and texts, with various meanings.

For example, one algorithm for looking up a word in the dictionary consists of opening the dictionary in the middle, comparing the word you are looking for with the median word, selecting the first or second half of the dictionary depending on if the word you are looking up is before or after the median word, opening it again in the middle, and so on, until you find the word you are looking up. This algorithm can solve one problem having to do with written symbols: letters. Other algorithms can add and multiply. They solve problems having to do with other written symbols: numbers. Such algorithms are called *symbolic.*

Computer scientists often limit the meaning of the word *algorithm* to these symbolic algorithms. With this limitation, we cannot take the history of algorithms further back than the invention of writing. However, we do know that the notion of algorithm is as old as writing itself, since the earliest known written records show that the first scribes were already using addition and multiplication algorithms to keep accounting records. In fact, writing was probably invented for this very purpose.

Algorithms and Mathematics

Mathematicians became interested in developing algorithms very early on. For example, an algorithm attributed to Euclid (c. 300 BCE) calculates the greatest common divisor of two whole numbers. This algorithm merits some discussion. Readers who find math annoying can skip ahead or read these lines as they would a somewhat esoteric poem.

An algorithm generally receives input, which provides the ingredients to be "kneaded." In the case of the Euclidean algorithm, this input consists of two non-zero whole numbers, a and b, such that a is greater than b, for example, 471 and 90. An algorithm generally produces an output. In the case of the Euclidean algorithm, the output is a whole number which is the greatest common divisor of the numbers a and b.

Applying the Euclidean algorithm to the numbers 471 and 90, for example, consists of:

> replacing the two numbers by 90 and 21,
> then by 21 and 6,
> then by 6 and 3,
> then by 3, which is the result.

At each step, the algorithm computes the remainder r of the division of a by b, then replaces a by b and b by r. Thus, as $471 = 5 \times 90 + 21$, the remainder of the division of 471 by 90 is 21. At the first step, the first number is replaced by 90 and the second by 21, and so on. However, there is one exception: when the remainder is zero, computation stops and the result is the number *b*. This is what happens in the last step. The number 6 is divided by the number 3, the remainder is zero, so the result is 3.

The notion of algorithm was also a primary concern of mathematicians of the Middle Ages, who introduced the Hindu-Arabic numeral system and its accompanying algorithms. Among them was the Arabic-speaking Persian mathematician Muhammad ibn Mūsā al-Khwārizmī, the ninth-century author of the *Book of Addition and Subtraction According to the Hindu Calculation*. The name Al-Khwārizmī means "who is from the region of Khwarezm," in what is now Uzbekistan, where he was born. This name gave us the word *algorithm*, which appears in French as early as 1230 in its archaic form, *augorisme*, and in Middle English as *algorism*.

Finding the Words

While algorithms apply naturally to mathematical objects, they also have a place in all human activities. The concept of algorithm is an all-purpose concept. We have already mentioned several examples of algorithms. Another example in a very different area will allow us to address a key issue: how to describe an algorithm.

Suppose we want to go from the Louvre Museum to the Eiffel Tower in Paris. To that, we first walk west along the Right Bank, then cross the Seine at the Passerelle Léopold Sédar Senghor, and then continue walking west along the Left Bank to the Eiffel Tower. We do this perhaps without even knowing we are using an algorithm, a procedure that takes us from the Louvre to the Eiffel Tower.

Google maps provides this algorithm in graphic form:

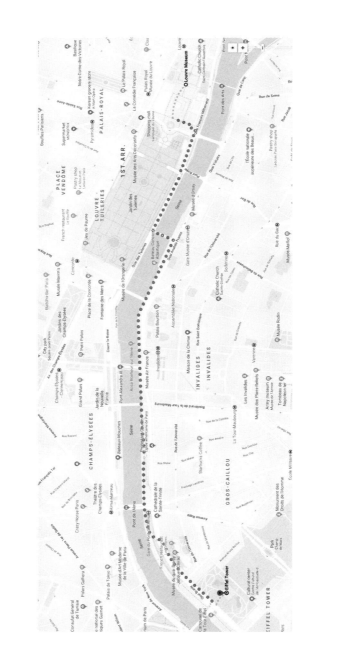

In text mode, the route begins with:

Google Maps   Louvre Museum to Eiffel Tower   Walk 3.5 km, 44 min

⚠ Use caution–walking directions may not always reflect real-world conditions

Louvre Museum
Rue de Rivoli, 75001 Paris, France

↑ 1. Head south on Cour Napoléon et Pyramide du Louvre
                                                              180 m

↱ 2. Turn right onto Quai François Mitterrand
                                                              280 m

↑ 3. Continue onto Quai Aimé Cesaire/Quai des Tuileries
                                                              400 m

↰ 4. Turn left onto Léopold Sedar Senghor
     ⓘ Take the stairs
                                                                5 m

↱ 5. Slight right to stay on Léopold Sedar Senghor
                                                               61 m

↰ 6. Turn left
                                                                5 m

↱ 7. Turn right
     ⓘ Take the stairs
                                                               73 m

↱ 8. Turn right
                                                              1.4 km

↱ 9. Slight right onto Voie Expresse Rive Gauche
                                                              550 m

↰ 10. Turn left toward Quai Branly
                                                               27 m

↱ 11. Turn right onto Quai Branly
                                                              550 m

Eiffel Tower
Champ de Mars, 5 Avenue Anatole France, 75007 Paris, France

These directions are for planning purposes only. You may find that construction projects, traffic, weather, or other events may cause conditions to differ from the map results, and you should plan your route accordingly. You must obey all signs or notices regarding your route.

If we were explaining this algorithm to a Parisian, we would be more concise. On the other hand, if we were explaining it to a visitor, we would provide more detail. The manner of expressing an algorithm has a social purpose that is dependent on those involved and their shared knowledge.

Likewise, the Euclidean algorithm can be expressed in text mode:

Compute the remainder r of the division of a by b, as long as r is not

equal to zero,
  replace a by b,
  replace b by r,
  compute the remainder r of the division of a by b,
the result is b.

Wikipedia also provides a graphic expression:

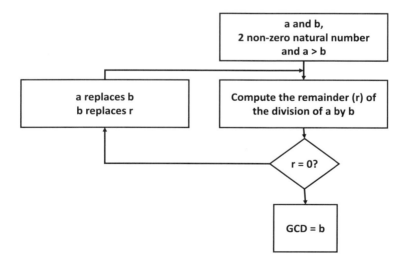

An algorithm can therefore be expressed in different languages, but it exists independently of these languages. A sleepy Parisian, heading to the Eiffel Tower on autopilot, can execute this algorithm without putting it in words. Another example provides an even better illustration of this last point, which can be confusing.

Ants looking for food use a very sophisticated spatial orientation algorithm. First, scout ants randomly walk around the anthill. When one of them finds a food source, it returns to the colony, leaving a trail of pheromones. Attracted to these pheromones, the ants nearby are encouraged to follow this trail. Returning to the anthill with food, they, in turn, leave pheromones which reinforce the trail.

If there are two possible trails to reach the same source of food, the ants that take the shorter route will make more round trips in the same amount of time than those who take the longer route. In doing so, they will leave more pheromones. The shorter trail will be even more reinforced, making it the more attractive choice. Since pheromones are volatile, the longer trail will eventually disappear.

So ant colonies use a complex algorithm to determine the shortest trail. And this procedure was used by ants long before it was described by myrmecologists.

What specifically distinguishes us from ants is that we attempt to describe, memorize, transmit, understand, and improve our algorithms. Even so, we also often use algorithms that we do not know how to describe. We can pretty easily distinguish between a dog and a cat. But it's difficult for us to explain how we do it. Do we start with the paws or the ears? Do we look at head shape or fur texture?

Our brains and our bodies, in order to see or move, use many algorithms, symbolic or not, that we cannot always explain.

Beyond Instruction Sequencing

The algorithm for going from the Louvre to the Eiffel Tower is expressed as a sequence of elementary actions such as: "head south on Cour Napoléon et Pyramide du Louvre," then, then, then. The expression of the Euclidean algorithm also includes elementary instructions such as the *assignment* "replace *a* by *b*," and constructions to link them together such as the *sequence* "do this, then that" and the *loop* "as long as this is true, repeat that." We could also add the *test*: "if this is true, do that."

It may seem surprising, but only a few constructions are necessary to express all of the symbolic algorithms. For example, these four constructions, assignment, sequence, loop, and test, are sufficient. The richness of algorithms does not come from the complexity of their components, but from the manner in which a few simple components are assembled.

The reader will be able to draw a parallel between the fact that the billions of known molecules are composed of only a few dozen chemical elements, themselves composed of three elementary particles: protons, neutrons, and electrons.

However, although these few ingredients are sufficient in theory, we rarely create algorithms starting from scratch. The ingredients of algorithms are often other already known algorithms. For example, we described an algorithm for going from the Louvre to the Eiffel Tower. If we now want to go from the Picasso Museum to the Eiffel Tower, a simple algorithm would be to walk from the Picasso Museum to the Louvre, and then to use the previous algorithm, viewed as a separate entity. In so formulating this new algorithm, we can ignore the details of the previous algorithm, choosing to view it as a new elementary instruction.

Algorithms and Data

The algorithms used to solve problems relating to symbolic information are very sensitive to the manner in which the information is presented. For example, there are much better algorithms for computing addition and multiplication for numbers written in Arabic numerals, 123 × 456, than for numbers written in Roman numerals, CXXIII × CDLVI. Likewise, looking up a word in a dictionary is easier in an alphabetical writing system than in an ideographic writing system.

Pathfinding algorithms for going from one point to another are also very sensitive to data representation. If a city map is presented pixel by pixel, like a photo, it is very difficult to navigate. It is more effective to describe it abstractly, as a series of intersections connected by streets, each one having a specific length. In this way, instead of laboriously plodding from pixel to pixel, the algorithm can jump from intersection to intersection.

Algorithmic Techniques

We know many algorithms. Quite a few algorithmic techniques underlie many of those, including *divide and conquer, generate-and-test, greedy algorithms*, or *randomization.*

The *divide and conquer* approach consists of solving a problem by breaking it down into two simpler problems; solving them, possibly by breaking them down again into two problems, and so on; then constructing the solution of the initial problem by combining the solutions of these two problems. Donald Knuth illustrates this technique using the example of mail distribution. Letters are sorted into separate stacks for each neighborhood of a city. Then, each mail carrier, responsible for a neighborhood, sorts the stacks into several smaller stacks for each building. Each building caretaker then sorts the stacks into smaller stacks for each of the apartments.

> ■ Donald Knuth--
>
> Donald Ervin Knuth (born in 1938) is one of the most influential computer scientists. One of the pioneers of modern algorithmics, his series *The Art of Computer Programming* has been an important reference for many years.
>
> Dissatisfied with the available word processing tools, he created the widely used TeX and Metafont open-source software programs.
>
> His name has been given to many well-known algorithms, including the Knuth–Morris–Pratt algorithm, Knuth's Algorithm X, Robinson–Schensted–Knuth algorithm, and the Knuth–Bendix completion algorithm.

The *enumerate and test* technique consists of solving a problem while listing all of the possible solutions and testing them one after the other. For example, when a traveling salesman has to visit clients in several towns, he will usually try to organize his route in such a way as to minimize the total distance traveled. An algorithm to determine the shortest route involves computing all of the possible routes – for example, for ten clients, there are 3,628,800 routes – by calculating the length of each and then choosing the shortest one.

Greedy algorithms find reasonable solutions to optimization problems when enumeration and test algorithms require too much computation. For example, a traveling salesman with twenty clients, using the enumerate and test technique, would have to test more than two billion billion possible routes. Rather than embark on such an exhaustive enumeration, a search algorithm can be used that goes from the closest town to the next closest, then to the town that is closest to the next closest town, and so on. Such an algorithm greedily absorbs the miles without ever questioning the previous choices. The resulting solution is not generally the best, but it is a "reasonable" one.

We have already seen an example of the use of randomization in an algorithm. To find food, scout ants begin by randomly walking around the anthill. Many other algorithms also use a random starting point. The Monte Carlo algorithm, for example, can determine the area of a complex figure within a square. Points are selected randomly in the square, for example, by throwing darts. According to the law of large numbers, these points will fall in the figure with a frequency close to the ratio of the area of this figure to that of the square.

Machine Learning

The last technique we'll discuss is *learning*. We're used to a person learning to bake bread or to look up a word in a dictionary, but it's more surprising to us that an algorithm can also learn. Just as a baker learns from experience and improves every day, an algorithm can learn by repeating the same task and improving.

An example of algorithms that can learn are the recommendation algorithms on music, video, and book platforms. Such systems make suggestions, such as "You liked *King Arthur*, perhaps you'll like *Peter Grimes*." To formulate this recommendation, the system is not based on its knowledge of the ties that unite Henry Purcell and Benjamin Britten. It is based, more simply, on the analysis of the selections previous users have listened to and on the fact that, among those who listened to *King Arthur*, there are many, in relative terms, who also listened to *Peter Grimes*. Alternatively, the algorithm can try to find users, most likely unknown to us, whose tastes are close to ours. In both cases, the algorithm learns, discovering statistical proximities between music pieces or between users. Based on this learning, the algorithm can predict what we will like, and therefore what we will be tempted to listen to or purchase.

These algorithms that learn provide a new way of looking at how we ourselves learn. Recommendation algorithms learn the ties that unite Purcell and Britten, without any expertise in music history. They simply observe our choices and learn from what they observe. This is not very different from how a child learns its native language by observing the people around her, by imitating them, and by spending a lot of time speaking, without any understanding of grammar, conjugation, or declensions. Just as a child knows that you shouldn't say "I gone to school," instead of "I went to school," but is unable to explain why, a recommendation algorithm will know to recommend Benjamin Britten without being able to explain why we might like this composer.

Certain learning problems are difficult to solve. If we try, for example, to recognize objects – a dog, a cat, a table – in an image, pixel by pixel, a statistical analysis that counts the number of black pixels or the number of blue pixels would have a difficult time distinguishing a dog from a table. We need to use more complex learning algorithms, *deep learning algorithms*, that first try to find shapes in the image – straight lines, circles, claws, paws, feet – and then increasingly complex objects. An algorithm constructs increasingly abstract representations of the image in this way, step by step, until the search items are recognized. One difficulty is to know which elements – claws, paws, feet, etc. – should be identified. The algorithm, however, can learn this on its own. Deep learning algorithms have been able to help programs that play Go improve to the point that they have beaten the best human players.

3

Algorithms, Computers, and Programs

We have been using symbolic algorithms since the advent of writing, five thousand years ago. How is it then that this concept has suddenly become such a hot topic in the public sphere today? To explain this, we need to look into objects other than algorithms – computers and programs.

Previously, the fears and fantasies around the role of computer science in our world revolved around the words *computers* and *robots*. It is only recently that we have seen a shift toward the word *algorithms*. It is no longer the computing objects and computers themselves that frighten us, but the fact that these objects *think*.

From Algorithms to Computers

One of the main benefits of algorithms, as we've said, is that they can be run mechanically. Once we have learned how to look up a word in the dictionary, to add, to compute the greatest common divisor of two numbers, or to make a diagnosis based on the results of a clinical examination, completing such tasks requires neither imagination nor talent. We simply have to apply the algorithm we have learned. This allows us to use our imagination and talent to do other things, for example, invent new algorithms.

Looking up a word in the dictionary, adding two numbers, and so on, are examples of tasks that can be carried out *automatically*. From this point to having a machine carry out such tasks rather than doing them ourselves, there is just one step, but one that took humankind five thousand years to make.

While the first machines, such as watermills, date back to ancient times, for a long time, algorithms and machines belonged to different cultural spheres. When Mesopotamian scribes invented the first algorithms for addition and multiplication, these algorithms were intended to be performed manually, by people, and not by machines. Similarly, the machines of Hero of Alexandria were used to run fountains, not to compute addition and multiplication.

The First Machines

It took time to develop the necessary techniques for machines to run symbolic algorithms. Abaci help us run algorithms, but since they do not compute on their own, they cannot be considered autonomous machines. The first machines capable of running symbolic algorithms were probably the bells of cathedrals, beginning in the late Middle Ages. Those of the Dijon cathedral, for example, included an automaton that rang a bell every hour. The Strasbourg cathedral clock included a statue of the Virgin before which the Three Kings bowed every hour, as well as a rooster that beat its wings. In addition, it calculated the position of the planets and the movable feast days.

These bells were followed in the seventeenth century by Schickard and Pascal's calculating machines, which could only add and subtract, and whose delicate clock mechanisms frequently jammed, and then by Leibniz's calculator which could also multiply and divide. These were followed in the eighteenth century by Vaucanson's automata, in the nineteenth century by the Falcon and Jacquard weaving looms and the Hollorith tabulating machine, and in the twentieth century, the Enigma and Leibniz machines, built just before the Second World War to encrypt and decrypt messages of the Axis powers, and the Bombe and Colossus machines built by the British to break the codes of these two machines, that is, to decipher the messages without knowing the key.

But none of these machines was yet a computer. While they did already possess some of the attributes of a computer, they lacked an essential quality: universality. Unlike an electric razor or mincer, which have only one function each, a computer is a versatile machine. A computer is also a universal machine that can run not only several, but all symbolic algorithms. It's literally an all-purpose machine. None of the machines we mentioned is universal.

This idea of universality appeared in the works of Ada Lovelace and Charles Babbage in the nineteenth century, but it was only fully understood by Alan Turing and Alonzo Church in the 1930s. And it was only in the 1940s that the first universal machines, that is, the first computers, were built. It's hard to say which exactly was the first universal machine: the Z3, built in Berlin; the ENIAC, built in Philadelphia; or Baby, built in Manchester, all in the 1940s. All three can legitimately lay claim to the title of the first computer in history.

This universality explains why computers are ubiquitous today, found in our workplaces managing the accounting, in our homes playing music and saving our vacation photos, in our cars guiding us through the intricacies of one-way streets, and so forth. This universality leads to a blurring of lines between various objects. We don't really have telephones, cameras, watches, or music players anymore. All of these functions are performed by a single object, a pocket computer that we arbitrarily call a "phone."

Shortly after the first computers were built, we learned to construct networks of connected computers, building increasingly complex computer systems. At the end of the twentieth century, computers had become inexpensive enough to be part of every home.

In the age of algorithms, when some people complain of the dehumanization of the world in which an insurance company determines the amount to be paid out to the victim of an accident using a *cynical algorithm*, they are not referring solely to the procedure by which the insurance company calculates this amount, but also to the machine, the computer, on which the calculation is carried out. The radical transformation of the world that we are experiencing today is not exclusively due to the invention of algorithms five thousand years ago but also to the invention of machines to run algorithms, computers, and to the development of a science and a technique, computer science, that this invention engendered.

Of Machines and Languages

To use an all-purpose machine, we have to indicate which algorithm we would like it to run, describing it in a specific language, called a *programming language*. The description of an algorithm in such a language is called a *computer program* or, simply, a *program*. For example, here is a program written in the programming language Java that specifies the Euclidean

■ Ada Lovelace--

The first computer programmer in history was a woman.

Ada Lovelace was born in London in 1815, and died in 1852. She was the daughter of the poet Lord Byron and the mathematician Annabella Milbanke. Ada Lovelace was one of the first computer scientists. We can say that she produced the first computer program written and published as such. This program was written for the analytical engine built by Charles Babbage. Beyond this calculator, Ada Lovelace was truly among the pioneers who envisioned a universal machine capable of running any symbolic algorithm.

The program that Ada Lovelace described in her notes calculated Bernoulli numbers. It's no surprise that it was a mathematical algorithm: algorithmics is rooted in mathematics and Ada Lovelace was herself a mathematician. More surprisingly, Ada Lovelace considered stepping out of the mathematical framework. She wrote that "the engine might compose elaborate and scientific pieces of music of any degree of complexity or extent."

The programming language Ada was named in her honor.

algorithm (see Chapter 2, section on "Algorithms and Mathematics"):

```
r = a % b;
while (r != 0) {
        a = b;
        b = r;
        r = a % b;
}
```

A program contains more information than the algorithm that it implements, because it specifies many details. For instance, that the numbers for which the computer finds the greatest common divisor must be requested from the user, who must type them on the keyboard or write them in a file; that the result must be shown on a screen or written in another file; that the program must use libraries written by others; that the data is represented in certain ways, and so on.

Digitized Information

Computers run algorithms only on symbolic data. However, we know that computers can also store, transmit, and transform images, sounds, and videos, which are not made up of symbols. How do they do this? They represent these images, sounds, or videos by a series of symbols that form an approximation of these "analog" forms of information.

In order to represent an image using a series of symbols, for example, we cut it into a finite number of rectangles, called *pixels*, and simplify each pixel by converting it to a mono-chromatic pixel, which is a first approximation, then we consider only a finite number of colors and assign a color from this palette to each pixel, which is the second approxi-mation. A photo generally contains several million pixels, each one of a color selected from a palette containing 16 million colors. With such values, our eye is incapable of discern-ing between a real – non-pixelated – image and one represented in a symbolic form. If we occasionally perceive that an image is pixelated, it's because we have not used enough pixels. The color of each pixel is represented by a

■ Bits, Bytes, Petabytes-------------------------------------

The basic unit for representing information is the *bit*. This is the information contained in a message formed by a symbol selected from a two-symbol alphabet, for example, 0 and 1. One bit is sufficient to say, "It's day" or "It's night." With three bits, we can form eight different messages: 000, 001, 010, 011, 100, 101, 110, 111. With three bits, we can express the days of the week, 000 for "Monday," 001 for "Tuesday," . . . 110 for "Sunday."

For historical reasons, we often use a derived unit, the *byte*, which is equal to eight bits. With eight bits, we can express 256 different messages. This is enough to choose a letter in an alphabet that contains the lower- and uppercase letters, accented vowels, numbers, and punctuation symbols used in languages with a Latin-derived alphabet, which amounts to about a hundred letters.

One thousand bytes form a *kilobyte*, 1,000 kilobytes a *megabyte*, 1,000 megabytes a *gigabyte*, 1,000 gigabytes a *terabyte*, 1,000 terabytes a *petabyte*. One petabyte is equal to 8 million billion bits. Is your head spinning yet?

To get an idea of the order of magnitude, the quantity of information included in a page of text is a few kilobytes; in a book, a few megabytes; in a small, thousand-volume library, a few gigabytes. The quantity of information included in all of the texts at the Library of Congress is a few terabytes; that produced by the European Organization for Nuclear Research (CERN) in one year is a few petabytes.

series of 24 bits. An image made up of 10 million pixels is represented as a series of 240 million bits, or 30 megabytes. (see box on "Bits, Bytes, Petabytes").

A digital camera transforms a real image that we see in the viewfinder into an image represented in symbolic form. This representation of the image can be stored, transmitted, and transformed. The camera is capable of running sophisticated algorithms on these images. Some of these algorithms could be performed on an analog image, that is, non-pixelated, but others are too complex to do so.

Sounds can also be represented in a symbolic manner, at the cost, here again, of an approximation. The notion of symbolic representation of sound is not completely new. Music notation represents a sound by splitting it into notes that have a pitch and a length selected from a finite range which also constitutes an approximation. Composers are well acquainted with the difficulty of transcribing the music of a locomotive or the song of a bluebird in this way.

A computer can process these representations of an image, a sound, or a video as a series of symbols. As the symbols used are generally numbers – and often only the numbers 0 and 1 – this representation of an image or video as a series of symbols is called the *digitization* of the image, sound, and so on. The resulting artifact is called *digital*. This is why the adjective *digital* is used to refer to the world in the age of algorithms. The fact of having digitized this information opens up a world of possibilities, making it possible to store images and sounds, to transmit, replicate, search, analyze, and transform them.

Varied and Universal

Thus, a computer can apply algorithms not only to symbolic information such as texts but also to digitized information such as images. It can also interact with the physical world, for example, control a dough mixer motor and make bread, if we equip it with an interface. In this way, computers have become embedded in trains, cars, airplanes, and tractors. It's only a slight exaggeration to say that a car is nothing more than a small network of computers equipped with a four-wheeled motor. Its onboard computers control everything: fuel injection, gear shifting, and braking. Another computer guides us to the tiniest village in the middle of nowhere and helps us avoid traffic jams using an external computer network that provides the latest traffic information.

In the same way, televisions, cameras, telephones, watches, music players, e-readers, and set-top boxes are computers, that is, universal machines that we have specialized to make them easier to use. The computer of a digital camera contains image processing programs that we don't find in an e-reader. However, digital cameras and e-readers contain processors that are universal machines. Although they appear to do very specialized, and very different, things, and while for some of these objects we have to make do with only the programs provided by the designers, these objects are all constructed around universal machines.

To appreciate the immense variety of these machines, let us consider the diversity of the things we call *robots*. In 1921, when it made its first appearance in Karel Čapek's play *R.U.R.*, the word *robot* referred to a humanoid machine. Today, we have domestic robots capable of helping us cook or do housework. Industrial robots are more sophisticated and highly specialized. Some are very powerful, others extremely precise. While R2-D2, C-3P0, and BB-8 of *Star Wars* still belong to the realm of science fiction, we are seeing the development of increasingly sophisticated humanoid robots, capable of independently performing *high-level* tasks such as playing soccer or dancing.

■ Edsger Dijkstra--

Edsger Dijkstra (1930–2002) was a Dutch computer scientist, one of the great pioneers of the field. He made fundamental contributions to the areas of programming languages, algorithm design, and distributed computing. An elegant algorithm that calculates the shortest path in a graph bears his name.

He is also famous for his strong personality, which some qualified as "difficult," and for his quotes, including, "testing shows the presence, not the absence of bugs," while "computer science is no more about computers than astronomy is about telescopes" has been incorrectly attributed to Dijkstra. In fact, two other computer scientists, Michael R. Fellows and Ian Parberry, most likely said it first.

Here is another difference. Apart from domestic computers, there are also computers that are "battery-raised" in "farms" of millions of computers, called *data centers*.

We are living in the midst of a bestiary of computers that are very different from each other, that have transformed, each in its own way, our personal and professional environments. Despite their differences, these computers remain intrinsically the same thing: universal machines.

We can also create computers in a variety of ways. Students in Lyon, France, and Aarhus, Denmark, among others, built a mechanical Turing machine out of Legos. Researchers are experimenting with other types of computers, taking their inspiration from living organisms. Others are attempting to exploit the laws of quantum physics to build computers in yet a different way.

4

What Algorithms Do

Algorithms and computers help with everything. But what tangible purpose do they serve? The remarkable diversity of their uses derives from their universality.

Computation

Historically, computers were first used for performing computation, in the meaning of the word before the invention of computers, that is, transforming data, typically numbers. Included in this class, for example, are algorithms that solve equations and encrypt or decrypt messages.

Information Management

It was soon obvious that computers could be used in another way: to store, query, and update large quantities of information, such as a library catalog or a company's client files. To a certain extent, the algorithms used are relatively simple. For example, looking up the title of a book in a catalog is no more complicated than looking up a word in the dictionary. However, the volume of data involved justifies the use of a computer, as does the fact that information must be protected, for example, against hardware failure, because it is of considerable value to the entire community of users.

Algorithms that archive data for long-term storage are also included in this category.

Communication

In contrast to the archiving function, which places information in a time capsule, certain algorithms transport information in space. This is the case for algorithms used for email. The information is not modified during transit, but efficiently moving information across a network of several billion computers requires complex algorithms and communication *protocols*, including the famous *Internet Protocol*.

Computer networks are slowly replacing postal, telephone, and television broadcasting networks. This convergence of computer science and telecommunications is perhaps the phenomenon that we least expected. In certain science-fiction novels of the 1960s, the inhabitants of Earth in the year 2000 travel in flying cars, but they stop at phone booths to make their calls.

Exploration

When we want to go from the Louvre to the Eiffel Tower as quickly as possible using public transportation, an algorithm can help us find the shortest path. When we need to find an efficient way of packing three thousand boxes into containers, an algorithm is indispensable for finding the best distribution.

Whether we're looking for the shortest path or the best distribution, these algorithms work in roughly the same way. They explore a large number of paths or box distribution combinations before choosing one. These are enumerate and test algorithms. When there are too many configurations to explore, they use heuristics, such as the greedy method, to avoid having to try them all.

Data Analysis

Statistical agencies, such as the US Congressional Budget Office, regularly forecast the growth of their respective country's gross domestic product. The information is obtained by data analysis algorithms that aggregate many indicators, such as sales indices, vehicle registrations, and international trade statistics.

Data analysis is increasingly used in scientific research. Image analysis, for example, can be used to automatically classify galaxies. Word frequency analysis in texts, such as of certain passages of the Bible, can aid in distinguishing between the authors. In our daily life, the choice of results that search engines suggest; recommendations for films, books, and partners; and the selection of ads that we see are based on the analysis of data gathered when we use its services. The development of the web and smartphones have contributed to the production of huge amounts of data that we have learned to analyze using massively parallel computers. This is the field of *big data*.

Signal Processing

Part of the information processed by algorithms comes from sensors that measure physical values such as temperature, pressure, and luminosity. The result of these measurements constitutes a *signal* that can depend on time or space. Sound, for example, is the variation of air pressure over time. Images are the variation of brightness in space.

A signal can be represented in analog form. For example, a pressure sensor, a microphone, transforms sound into an electrical signal. The electrical intensity variation is the analog of the pressure variation. A digital microphone, in contrast, transforms sound into a series of numbers, that is, into a series of symbols.

The electrical signal representing the sound can be amplified or transformed by specialized devices. The same signal represented digitally can be treated by algorithms and computers.

Changing the mode of representation of sounds and images can greatly alter how this information is processed. For example, film cameras use a complex system of lenses to guide each light beam to a precise point on the negative, without which the image would be deformed. A photographed straight line would appear in the photo as a curved line. There is no need for such a lens in a digital camera, made up of a few million light sensors. If the light beam hits the wrong spot, an algorithm can correct the distortion. Since digital cameras do not require complex lenses, they are much less expensive than their film counterparts. So much so that these days, we always have one in our pocket.

Using universal machines, computers, rather than specialized machines for signal processing, has also contributed to the decrease in processing costs. In the twentieth century, musicians just starting out spent a fortune on studio access to produce their first albums. Now, with a digital microphone, an ordinary computer, and signal processing software, they can obtain a quality close to that of a professional studio.

Camcorders, cameras, microphones, computers, and signal processing software have brought tools previously reserved for professionals within everyone's reach.

Object Control

Algorithms that control objects often use information from sensors. For example, the algorithm behind self-driving cars processes not only the information provided by the passenger, essentially the desired destination, but also information provided by the various cameras on the vehicle that allow it to evaluate road conditions.

These algorithms must often compute in real time. When the light turns red, the algorithm not only has to activate the car brakes, but it must do so instantly and not a few seconds later.

Manufacturing

Algorithms are used to automate the production of material objects in factories where raw materials enter at one end and finished objects exit at the other end. Each machine is controlled by an algorithm, and the overall production is overseen by other algorithms. The objects that are produced this way, like smartphones, are of a complexity incomparable to twentieth-century telephones.

There are still some people present in these factories to check that the machines are working properly and to repair them if necessary, but compared with nineteenth- and twentieth-century factories, these factories are largely devoid of human beings.

Modeling and Simulation

The keystone of our understanding of the world is the construction of theories: Newtonian mechanics, relativity, evolution, and so on. A theory is called *scientific* when it can be used to make predictions that can be compared with observations.

For example, Newtonian mechanics allows us to predict well in advance when the sun will rise and set at a point on the globe. We can then compare the predicted time with the actual time observed. If these two times do not coincide, there is a problem with the theory.

Some theories can be formulated using algorithms, such as an algorithm for calculating planetary movement in the solar system. Such algorithmic theories are called *models*. Because of their algorithmic character, a computer can use these models to *simulate* the modeled phenomenon. We have developed models of many phenomena – changes in oceans and atmosphere, brain function, tectonic plate movement, urban development, stock market variation, and crowd movement, to name a few.

Traditional theories were based on a small number of equations. The equations of Newtonian mechanics take up only a few lines. Models using algorithms can construct much more complex theories involving a large number of very diverse aspects. For example, an urban development model must take into account various demographic, economic, political, and geographic processes that interact with each other. Because of this complexity, certain phenomena can be modeled and simulated without being fully understood. Newtonian physicists could master their equations, follow the reasoning step by step, and interpret the result. The complexity of a weather model, for example, makes it impossible to follow all of the computations and to succinctly explain the result. Such a model allows us to confidently predict whether or not it will rain tomorrow, but it cannot tell us why.

In principle, models are subject to the same constraints as other theories. The predictions should be in agreement with the observations; otherwise, they are incorrect. That said, due to their complexity, we need to take another look at the meaning of the word *incorrect*. When the predictions of a traditional theory did not match the observations, the theory had to be abandoned, or at least fundamentally overhauled. But when the predictions of a complex model, dependent on many parameters, are in *slight* disagreement with certain observations, we're not going to *throw out* the model. Instead, we'll try to correct it by slightly modifying the value of one of its parameters to bring it more in line with the observations. If the differences are too great, we can try to increase the complexity slightly by introducing a new factor, so that the model is not considered completely defective and has to be discarded. When the predictions differ from the observations, attempts are made to improve it. As a result, algorithmic models place us in a paradoxical situation. By making it possible to study phenomena that are much more complex than traditional theories, they lead to an extension of the reach of science. However, because of the difficulty in explaining results and in comparing predictions with the observations, they may result in a potential weakening of scientific rigor.

Different types of algorithms described in this chapter often cooperate within the same system. In a driverless train, for example, some algorithms control the speed of the train, and others the regulation of traffic. This panorama illustrates the richness of our algorithmic heritage that we are constantly enriching by improving known algorithms or creating new ones.

5

What Algorithms Don't Do

A lgorithms are often disparaged, but they are also sometimes overrated. To understand their place in our world it
is also important to understand their limits.

The Limits of Computation

The work of mathematicians of the 1930s, such as Jacques
Herbrand, Kurt Gödel, Alonzo Church, Alan Turing, Stephen
Kleene, and Emil Post, revealed a class of problems that could
be solved with algorithms. It may seem surprising, but this
class is independent of the language used to describe algorithms (see Chapter 2, section on "Finding the Words").
We can choose languages that are very different and yet they
all express this same class of problems, reinforcing the idea that
algorithms are independent of the language in which they are
described.

The problems that we can solve with an algorithm are called
computable or *decidable*. In contrast, problems for which this is
not possible are *not computable*, or *undecidable*. The idea
might be disturbing, but even if all of the programmers in the
world were brought together to solve one of these problems,
there would be no chance of success.

Without providing here a proof of the existence of such
problems, we can suggest a reason why certain problems are
undecidable. Imagine a group of children on a treasure hunt in

the countryside. The first clue instructs them to go to the apple tree, where they find a second clue which tells them to go to the barn, where they find a third clue which tells them to do something else, and so on. The children follow a rather unpredictable path that leads them from south to north and from north to south, perhaps quite far from their starting point.

We can easily answer the question of whether the children will find the magic wand during the first five steps of the treasure hunt. For that, we ourselves simply follow the messages for five steps to find out if they lead us to a magic wand or not. The question of whether the children find the magic wand before the end of the treasure hunt is much more difficult, but can still be answered. For that, we must follow the clues until we either find the magic wand or finish the treasure hunt without having found it.

In any case, this method allows us to answer the question only because we know that the treasure hunt has an end. It would be unreasonable to suppose that the organizers of the treasure hunt bothered to leave an infinite number of clues.

Imagine now that an infinite treasure hunt is possible. For example, we leave home and follow the indications of an algorithm that, given our location on Earth, decides our next destination. Let's ask ourselves if our road leads to Rome or not. We can try to answer this question using the same method as in the first treasure hunt and go from one stage of the journey to the next asking ourselves at each stop if we've arrived in Rome. It's possible that we would get there in five stages, or in ten, but it's also possible that we would wander forever, from stage to stage, without ever reaching Rome. In addition, we wouldn't have any means of knowing if we would actually arrive one day or if we would just wander forever. The only thing we could do is to go to the next stage.

■ Alan Turing--

Alan Turing (1912–1954) was a brilliant British mathematician and computer scientist.

Early in his career, he invented the Turing machine, an elegant mathematical model of a computer, which enabled him to take part in the construction of the Church–Turing thesis, contributing to the concept of *computable* problems.

During the Second World War, he helped break the secret German code of the Enigma machine. This work was of considerable importance in leading the Allies to victory.

After the war, he conducted research on the first computers. He developed an artificial intelligence test, the *Turing test*, based primarily on the ability of a program to deceive a human by presenting itself as human.

During his last years, he made important contributions to biology in his work on morphogenesis in nature.

In 1952, legal charges were brought against him because of his homosexuality. Turing agreed to chemical castration to avoid prison. He was found dead from cyanide poisoning in his Manchester home on June 7, 1954, most likely by suicide.

It would take more than fifty years for him to be rehabilitated and recognized as a hero of the Second World War.

We often encounter undecidable problems when we try to create programs that transform other programs. For example, a *compiler* is a program that translates a program written by a human into another program that is executable directly by a computer. In general, compilers try to produce shorter programs by removing unused program code. However, this problem is undecidable. There is no algorithm that can determine if a particular piece of code is useful or not. For this, compilers use heuristics to eliminate certain pieces of unused code, but we cannot guarantee that they have not let others slip through.

Computation Time

Fortunately, the problems that we encounter in our daily life are usually computable. However, we often encounter problems that, while computable, can be solved only by algorithms that require an extravagant amount of computing time, rendering them unsolvable in practice.

Just as geographers attempt to measure the height of mountains and the length of rivers, computer scientists attempt to measure the *complexity* of problems they encounter, that is, the time that an algorithm needs to solve them.

Earlier, we discussed the problem of the traveling salesman who must visit his clients in various cities and wants to organize his route to minimize the total distance traveled. In a variation of this problem, he simply tries to identify a route that is, for example, less than 500 miles. The algorithm that lists all of the possible routes and then tests them one after the other requires an astronomically long computation time: 3,628,800 routes to test for ten clients, more than two billion billion for twenty clients, and so on. The number of routes and, therefore, the computation time, grows exponentially with the number of clients. This algorithm can be used in practice only if the number of clients is very small.

The existence of a rapid algorithm for deciding if there exists a route of a given maximum length has been an open problem for more than forty years. It has been listed as one of the seven

Millennium Prize Problems of the Clay Institute, which is offering a prize of one million dollars for its solution. The name of this problem is $P \neq NP$ (i.e., P does not equal NP). The class P is, in fact, the class of problems that can be solved quickly, and the class NP, to which the traveling salesman problem belongs, consists of problems whose solutions can be quickly verified once they have been found. For example, once a route has been established, it can be quickly verified that the route is indeed shorter than 500 miles. If we can prove that $P = NP$, that will show that there does exist an algorithm, yet to be discovered, that can rapidly solve our variant of the traveling salesman problem. If we can prove that $P \neq NP$, we won't have to worry about finding such an algorithm, because it does not exist!

Other Resources

While computing time is traditionally in short supply, other resources can also limit the use of algorithms and computers to solve problems, such as computer memory, which stores information, or the energy dissipated by computation. This last resource is often scarce and expensive, for example, for phones that must run on a small battery. We also have to take into account the development time of the algorithm and of the program that specifies it.

All of these reasons make it sometimes impossible to solve a problem with an algorithm. Algorithms are not the solution to all of our problems.

Reliability

It is possible that your telephone may mistakenly send a flirtatious text message to your grandmother rather than the intended recipient. Algorithms can contain errors. Software and material components can also malfunction.

These *bugs* are not limited to computer systems. Experienced pilots can also commit errors that lead to catastrophes. These errors are relatively common in computer systems, because they are the most complex things that man has created. A bicycle is typically made up of around one hundred mechanical parts; the operating system of a telephone, ten million lines of programs. Due to the complexity of such computer systems and the sometimes increasingly short periods of development, we should almost be surprised that in general, they do function correctly.

These bugs are not all of the same magnitude. When the application that provides the bus schedule on our telephone doesn't work, we can obtain the same information by looking it up on a website or by going to the bus stop. When we are in an airplane piloted by a software program or when we are operated on by a robot surgeon, we go so far as to put our lives in the hands of an algorithm. If the program that controls a nuclear power plant does not function correctly, it can have disastrous consequences.

In critical areas, such as transportation, health, and energy, we make a special effort to eliminate bugs. Even if an automatic pilot, for example, makes fewer errors than a flesh and bone pilot, in these critical areas, that's not enough. We are more demanding of computer systems than of human beings in such areas.

Part of computer science research is dedicated to the design of methods for avoiding bugs and thus building a kind of trust in algorithms. These methods are quite diverse. They deal as much with the management of coding teams and the design of test methods as with program analysis. Program analysis consists of having a person, who is often different from the one who wrote the program, reread the program, and try to understand it or even demonstrate that the program verifies the properties stated in its specifications.

We have seen that one algorithm for looking up a word in the dictionary consists of opening it in the middle, choosing the first or the second half depending on whether the word being looked up comes before or after the median word, opening it in the middle, and so on, until the word is found. For example, when we look up the word *abalone* in a dictionary made up of ten words – *aardvark, aardwolf, aba, abaca, aback, abacterial, abacus, abaft, abalone, zymurgy* – the first step selects the list *abacterial, abacus, abaft, abalone, zymurgy*, the second the list *abalone, zymurgy*, and the third finds the word *abalone*.

The specification of such an algorithm requires that, if the words are listed in alphabetic order in the dictionary, and if the searched for word is in the dictionary, the algorithm must find it. To demonstrate that the algorithm verifies this property, we show that at each step, the size of the list is reduced, and if the searched word belongs in the initial list, it will belong to the selected list. The word *demonstrate* here has the same meaning as in logic and in mathematics.

Of course, rather than demonstrating themselves that the programs verify the properties required in the specifications, computer scientists seek to have other programs demonstrate it for them.

It is thus possible to eliminate many bugs from programs and to considerably increase their reliability. However, despite all of these precautions, it does happen that certain bugs escape us, for instance, when the specifications themselves contain an error. Perfection is not attainable and zero error does not exist. We can only do our best to make sure it happens as rarely as possible.

When errors do occur, the program should nevertheless continue to run, even if only in a degraded mode. For example, if a server breaks down, the duplication of service on another machine will prevent an interruption in service.

The demand for perfection comes at a price. The price is justified in the case of the automatic pilot of an airplane or in a self-driving car. We must accept that the development of such systems takes a lot of time and the costs are high. In other cases, for example, for free applications of relative usefulness, the desire to get the service up and running as soon as possible takes precedence over reliability. This is often what leads to poor quality software, which is by itself no more and no less to blame than the cheap kite that tears in the first blast of wind.

Security

Security is a very different problem than reliability, but it also places a limit on the use of algorithms. If an airplane crashes because the engine failed, there is a reliability problem. If it crashes because a terrorist put a bomb on it, there is a security problem.

For a computer system, security is the ability to withstand attacks from malicious individuals attempting to take control of or access information that it not intended for them. The security of computer systems relies heavily on encryption methods.

When a website is not secure, a hacker can take control of it and change the information disseminated by the site. If a company's computer system is not secure, a competitor can steal the perfume formula the company is developing. We are witnessing a war between *white hat* hackers, security experts who protect computer systems, and *black hat* hackers, who look for weaknesses in these systems in order to attack them.

This war moves into the political sphere when, for example, a computer worm is used to attack Iranian nuclear facilities, or when hacktivists such as Julian Assange publish confidential public records.

Interaction with Humans

A final limit is the difficulty of dialogue between a human and an algorithm.

Air France Flight 447 from Rio to Paris crashed into the Atlantic Ocean. Human factors appear to have played a decisive role in the accident and, in particular, the interface between the pilots and the computers. It seems that the human pilots did not correctly interpret the data presented by the computers.

The question of the interaction between humans and algorithms, although it does not always have such dramatic consequences, is often the cause of failure in the use of computer systems. Many of our readers remember pulling out their hair when confronted with a user-unfriendly interface.

Too often, we must adapt to machines when it is they that should adapt to us. Human–machine interaction, however, is constantly improving, as shown, for example, by our telephone interfaces.

6

Computational Thinking

A scientific revolution does not only create new knowledge. It also generates new ways of thinking, new ways of asking questions, and new ways of answering them. Before the scientific revolution at the beginning of the seventeenth century, when questions were raised, for example, about whether or not blood circulated in the body, people looked for answers in the ancient texts. Aristotle and Galen taught that blood did not circulate in the body; therefore, the question had been answered. How did Aristotle and Galen know what they knew? That question was not posed. They were more knowledgeable than us, and that was sufficient.

This way of answering questions was abandoned little by little by the beginning of the seventeenth century and two new methods appeared – mathematization and observation. When Galileo observed with his telescope, in contradiction with the theory of orbs, four satellites orbiting Jupiter, or when William Harvey discovered that blood circulated in the human body by observing that blood flow varies when the tourniquet on an injured arm is tightened or loosened, they contributed not only new knowledge but also new ways of asking questions and new ways of answering them.

The computer revolution also brings with it new ways of thinking. The general term often used for these ways of thinking is *computational thinking*, or *algorithmic thinking*, which are more or less synonymous. This way of thinking, initially developed by computer scientists, is contaminating, or enriching, all of our ways of thinking. Like computer science, computational thinking has several dimensions.

The Use of Tools for Thinking

The most obvious of these dimensions is the use of databases, spreadsheets, and search engines to think.

For example, to answer the question, "What will the weather be like tomorrow?" meteorologists now enter into a computer thousands of measurements of temperature, pressure, wind speed, and so on, and then they use software to predict the movement of masses of air in the atmosphere and, finally, tomorrow's weather. Such a computation is too long to complete by hand, so this question cannot be answered accurately without a computer.

Everything Is Information Exchange

Computational thinking also leads to seeing many phenomena as exchanges of information between agents.

For example, what is a twenty-dollar bill? It is primarily information, stating that its bearer worked for an hour – or won the lottery – and it comes with the right to drink twenty coffees. This information is represented by a rectangle of paper. It could also be represented by a shell, a gold coin, or almost nothing – a few bits in a disc.

The Algorithmic Form of Knowledge

In response to a question that begins, "Do we know ...?" computer scientists often respond by describing an algorithm.

For example, in response to the question, "Do we know how to distinguish between a cancerous tumor and a benign one?" they might suggest an algorithm that can distinguish between two images. This algorithmic form of knowledge, which is at the heart of computational thinking, steers knowledge toward action. There has been a semantic shift from the ability to distinguish between a cancerous tumor and a benign tumor to the ability to formulate an algorithm to perform this task. Such algorithmic knowledge is necessary if we want to use a computer to analyze medical images, making it possible to analyze thousands of images, for example, during routine screening.

From data analysis to simulation, the richness of the algorithmic approach to problem solving never ceases to amaze us. Computational thinking has already transformed scientific research in a wide variety of fields, from biology to the digital humanities.

An Abundance of Languages

Ask a computer scientist to describe a text in which some words are in bold and others in italics, and she'll instantly come up with a language. For example, in the HTML language, the text, "**The** small *cat* is dead," is written "The small <i>cat</i> is dead". Such languages allow us to communicate with computers.

Even before the beginnings of computer science, we recognized the value of using languages for writing numbers, music, or aircraft records. These languages are obviously different from the language of the poems of T. S. Eliot. With computer science, the number of these languages has exploded.

The Coexistence of Different Levels of Abstraction

Computer scientists have also made a habit of observing the same objects at different levels of abstraction or according to abstractions associated with different points of view.

From a mechanic's point of view, a car is made up of components including an engine, a clutch, and a gearbox, while this breakdown is not useful for a police officer directing traffic. The mechanic and the police officer view the car at different levels of abstraction. The police officer, who takes fewer details into account, has a *higher level of abstraction* with respect to the car than the mechanic.

In the same way, a banknote can be seen as a piece of paper, an amount of money, or an information vector. These three descriptions are all accurate, but they lie at different levels of abstraction.

Computer scientists have gotten used to juggling multiple levels of abstraction at once. They view the same circuit board as a system of transistors in the morning, and as a set of logic gates at noon, and as the implementation of an algorithm in the evening. This is why, when faced with a new problem, the first thing a computer scientist does is try to find the right level of abstraction to describe it.

The technical activities of the past, like ceramics and carpentry, required, above all, a high level of manual dexterity. With computer science, new technical areas are emerging, such as programming or circuit design, where the ability to work at different levels of abstraction is more important than manual dexterity.

Women in Computer Science

We end this chapter with a popular misconception that we unfortunately have to fight against every day: that this way of thinking is somehow specific to the male gender.

Indeed, for years now, we have observed women's disenchantment with computer science and a decline in the number of women pursuing studies in this area. Too few women are studying science in general, and computer science in particular. However, those who do embark on these adventures are quite successful.

There are multiple reasons why computer science does not attract women in many countries. Beginning in elementary school, prejudices keep girls away from the sciences. We need to move away from the stereotypical view of the young male computer scientist, pathologically self-absorbed, subsisting on Coke and cold pizza. Computers scientists are more than that. This cliché, propagated by literature and film, definitely does not appeal to women. Finally, we have to admit that women are sometimes poorly received by their male colleagues, some of whom fear the feminization of their profession. These are some of the reasons that have been suggested, among others. But we have to recognize that the reasons for this disaffection are still poorly understood.

However, it's enough to observe history and geography to realize that it is completely unfounded. Ada Lovelace and Grace Hopper are highly regarded among the pioneers of computer science. There were many women in laboratories such as Bletchley Park and the Moore School, where the first computers were built. In some countries, like Malaysia, women now make up the majority of workers in information technology companies.

We see this disenchantment and we abhor it. We are working to make the computer science environment more welcoming to everyone, but results are still limited. Prestigious universities such as UC Berkeley and Carnegie Mellon have succeeded in changing the situation and increasing the number of women in the field. Success is possible!

— *Now, do you understand what an algorithm is?*
— *I think so, Robot. You were right, it's great!*
— *They're going to replace people to carry out the most tedious tasks.*
— *But if people don't have anything to do, how will they earn a living?*
— *They'll need to do a better job of sharing the wealth.*
— *Everything will go to the ones who possess the algorithms?*
— *Um . . ., that's exactly what we should avoid.*

7

The End of Employment

The Hitchhiker and the Pencil Sharpener

In 2002, during a performance/installation, *35 Hours of Work*, Benjamin Sabatier sharpened pencils seven hours a day for five days. Sharpening pencils in this way for thirty-five hours is a deviant act, because custom dictates that we use a pencil sharpener for a few seconds, to sharpen a pencil, after which we put it away in a drawer until we need it again. As a consequence, a pencil sharpener is used only a few minutes per year.

If each person in California wanted to own a pencil sharpener in order to use it for, let's say, one hour per decade, we would need about forty million pencil sharpeners. In fact, Californians purchase several million of them each year. But fewer than five hundred communal pencil sharpeners, used continuously, would suffice.

What is true for pencil sharpeners is true, to varying degrees, for many other objects, such as drills, bicycles, or lawn mowers. There are, of course, exceptions: objects that are made to be used continuously, such as pacemakers, or objects that are too personal to be shared, like toothbrushes.

We can ask ourselves why we produce millions of pencil sharpeners when a few hundred would suffice. The usual explanation is that the use of a communal object has an additional cost. For example, even if a single pencil sharpener would be sufficient, in theory, for a city with a population of 100,000, going across town each week in order to sharpen your pencils at the library would have a cost in terms of time and transportation that would greatly exceed that of the purchase of your own personal pencil sharpener. Likewise, while it is possible to do your laundry at a laundromat, or even through a website that can put you in touch with neighbors who will let you use their washing machine for a fee, the norm, in our country, is that each house or building typically has its own machine. Only a product cost that is significantly higher than the additional cost of sharing would make us deviate from the rule. Hence, pencil sharpeners and cars are personal objects, but airplanes are shared objects.

This balance, however, is threatened by the decrease in the additional cost of using shared objects, itself due to the use of algorithms to process information.

The use of communal cars in the form of car rentals, for example, has been in existence for a long time. In order to rent a car, you go to a specific parking lot where such cars are parked and fill out paperwork with the personnel of the rental agency. This takes time, as does picking up the keys and returning the vehicle. Because of the time spent by the two parties, car rentals have traditionally been expensive and relatively rare. Rather than rent a car each time we need to go somewhere, we prefer to own our own car. This is why a country or a state may have millions of cars when much fewer would suffice. All of the tasks completed when renting a car involve information exchange – signing the rental agreement, signing the insurance agreement, filling out a damage report when the car is rented or returned, or even the key exchange – that incorporates the information concerning the identity of the car user at a given moment. The processing of this information can now be done by algorithms, which leads to car sharing services, like Zipcar, that allow users to rent cars for short periods of time. Without computers or algorithms, the cost of such a system in time and in personnel would be exorbitant.

A good is *communal* when a process of information exchange allows people who do not know each other to share it. The owner of the good may be a company, as in the case of Zipcar. But nothing prevents an object from being, at the same time, partially communal and the property of an individual, even if this requires a more complex exchange of information. In this way, carpooling renders individually owned cars partially communal. Again, carpooling is old, and the carpooling of the twentieth century, called hitchhiking at the time, had an enormous additional cost – the hours spent on the side of the road in order to transmit the information to the drivers: "I'm here. I'm looking for a ride to Anchorage." Again, this information processing, more complex because it involves more participants, can be done at a lower cost by an algorithm for connecting people.

What is true for bicycles and cars, which are manufactured objects, is also true for other "objects," such as space. The average volume of a home is a few thousand cubic feet. However, the occupants of such a home use this portion of space barely half the time. They are out all day long, at work, at school, at daycare, and so on, and sometimes, they go on vacation, while at the same time, tourists visiting their city occupy hotels. Office space, even open space, is also poorly utilized. It is empty at night and often during the day as well, when its occupants are on vacation or working outside the company. Isn't there a better way to use space?

With telecommuting, the age of algorithms has created, for some professions, the possibility of working from home, which is a first step toward a better use of space. Telecommuting also reduces transportation time and, in theory, would allow people to do several tasks concurrently, such as work and, for young parents, childcare. It has become very common in certain professions, not surprisingly first and foremost in information technology companies, even if there are also some drawbacks, like the breakdown of boundaries between professional and personal life.

For the management of space, as for that of a car, the additional cost of sharing is the cost of information processing, which decreases when this information is processed by algorithms. With telecommuting, our home becomes an office space, it turns into a hotel when we rent it to tourists, a store when we make online purchases, and a pizzeria when we order a pizza.

But, more than a better utilization of pencil sharpeners, cars, or space, it is perhaps the management of work time that could benefit the most from low-cost information processing.

Managing Work Time

Companies sometimes need to translate a document from one language to another because their clients or their employees are located in different countries. A company has the choice of looking for a translator each time a translation is needed, or of employing a translator full-time. The choice naturally depends on the volume of documents to translate, but also on the ease of finding a translator. If the company has a regular need for translations, it is not cost effective to send out a call for availability, wait for translators to respond by email, write back to discuss pricing and delivery, and so on, every time the need arises. It is in the interests of the company to hire a translator even if she is sometimes paid to do nothing when there are not enough documents to translate.

However, if, as is the case today, it is enough to type "translation agency" into a search engine to find the website of a translator who receives the documents by email and sends them back in the same way, the company has every incentive to use the services of an independent translator whenever it has the need, rather than do all the paperwork and pay all the taxes necessary to employ a full-time translator who would be paid, at least part of the time, to do nothing.

Although the actors are different, the process is fundamentally the same in the communal use of a car and of a pencil sharpener. The lower costs of information processing allow for a better use of the resources, the car and the pencil sharpener in one case, and the work time of the translator in the other.

This observation has led some to predict that the lower costs of information processing could spell the end of employment and its replacement by another organization of work where each task to be accomplished would be the subject of a one-time contract. In other words, the salaried employment model of the nineteenth and twentieth centuries would have been only a temporary means of compensating for the inefficiency of information processing. However, others stress the limited scope of this switch from salaried work to self-employment. While certain company tasks can be outsourced, others require expertise acquired within the company, teamwork, or complex organization. For the company, outsourcing may lead to a loss in quality and expertise. While salaried employment may still have a future, it remains to be seen in which cases it will disappear and in which cases it will persist.

Our translator, previously a salaried employee, and now an independent contractor, also gains, in theory, a certain form of freedom. She no longer has to submit to the authority of a petty boss, she is not required to work every day from 9 to 6, she can accept as many or as few translation jobs as she wants based on her needs and desires. How is it then that translators, taxi drivers, journalists, and others, having become independent contractors, are often nostalgic for the time when they were salaried employees?

It is likely not the end of the restrictive employment conditions that they miss, but the loss of certain advantages that came with it. The status of salaried employee allows work to be exchanged for money, but it is also insurance against uncertainty, and in particular against income uncertainty. Imagine two translators, one translating into Portuguese and the other into Swedish. If, in a particular month, the only translation jobs are into Portuguese, the first translator will work and the other won't. If, the next month, the only translation jobs are into Swedish, it will be the second translator's turn to work. If the two translators are both independent contractors, one of them will have income the first month and the other the second. But if they are salaried employees, they will receive the same salary each month. In other words, salaried employment is a way for the two translators to provide for each other.

Other than this sharing of gains and losses, salaried employment is accompanied by other forms of insurance. For example, a company that pays salaries to employees is required by law to contribute to employee health insurance and retirement plans.

Finally, salaried employment allows employees to join forces in their dealings with the company, for example, in pay negotiations. It is more difficult for two independent contractors, a Brazilian and a Sami, to work together to better negotiate rates with the companies that employ them, even more so because rates vary according to location. While their organizing might one day be enhanced by the same communication techniques that now undermine salaried employment, the transformation of salaried work into self-employed work is often accompanied by an increase in precariousness for the workers.

Disillusion

How can we prevent an increase in the vulnerability of entire populations excluded from salaried or even direct part-time employment?

In some cases, it might be enough to show that digitization is just a pretext for eliminating social advantages. For example, the so-called independence of ride-hailing drivers is more appearance than reality. Uber allocates rides, sets rates, and determines revenue sharing. It is not very different from the taxi companies it claims to replace. The California Labor Commission recently ruled that an Uber driver was not an independent contractor, but an employee, which imposes a certain number of constraints on the company employing him.

However, in reinstating the status of employee for ride-hailing service drivers, the California Labor Commission skirts the real question: How to provide independent contractors with the same safeguards against uncertainty, the same sharing of gains and losses, the same health insurance, and the same rights to social security as employees?

For that we will need other structures to take over the role that companies traditionally played. The law could, for example, require individuals or companies that use the services of a driver or an independent translator to pay a share of social charges, similar to the payroll taxes contributed by companies on behalf of their employees to fund their social security and health insurance. Algorithms could manage the complexity of this type of system.

However, one obstacle that remains is the mismatch between the geography of laws and that of work.

We can also imagine a group of independent contractors, ride-hailing drivers, for example, creating their own cooperative which would assume the role of protecting against uncertainty, providing health insurance, and so forth. Such initiatives are beginning to emerge.

An important aspect of policy development in the twenty-first century will no doubt be the invention of new forms of social organizations that offer alternatives to both wage-based employment and precariousness, since the model of salaried, and even hourly, employees is on its way out.

8

The End of Work

In using the example of the professions of driver and translator, we implicitly assumed that drivers and translators would always exist. However, it is also possible that these professions may one day disappear if, at some point, algorithms for driving a car or translating a text perform as well as, or even better, than a human. This is also true for many other professions. Of course, this transition also paves the way for new professions to design, implement, and accompany all of these algorithms, but in the age of algorithms, much less work may be required to provide the same goods or services as before.

Because of this reduction in the quantity of work necessary to accomplish many tasks, we should question the robustness of the very concept of work as we understand it today. This is the view put forward in 2016, by Andrew Ng, scientific director of the Chinese company Baidu. "The rise of steam power and manufacturing left many out of work, but also created new jobs and entirely new fields that no one at the time could have imagined. This sea change took place over two centuries; America had time to adapt. Farmers tilled their fields until retirement, while their children went off to school and became electricians, factory foremen, real-estate agents, and food chemists. Truck drivers won't be so lucky. Their jobs, along with millions of others could soon be obsolete."

A Brief History of Technology and Work

Since prehistoric times, women and men have used tools, spears, hooks, nets, grindstones, sickles, and hammers to ease their work in carrying out the tasks necessary for their survival. Compared with hook-and-line fishing, a net can catch more fish in a shorter amount of time. However, a certain amount of work is required to make the net. A fisherman who makes a net gives up, initially, a certain amount of work to make the net in order to later be able to catch more fish with less effort. In this sense, tools constitute *capital*.

Some tools, such as watermills, use an external energy source which allows them a certain degree of autonomy and, for this reason, are called *machines*. Such machines have been used extensively since the end of the eighteenth century to make objects, fabrics, ceramics, and the like, that had previously been made by hand.

In the nineteenth and twentieth centuries, a period of transition, these objects were still made by people, with the assistance of machines, in factories. Workers surely thought they were using the machines, but, in practice, the workers often adapted themselves to the machines, according to the principles of Taylorism.

We gradually moved away from Taylorism in the second half of the twentieth century with full plant automation and the demise of assembly line work. The time is not far off when, to manufacture a car, you will only need to place a few cubes of material, metal, and plastic at one end of a fully automated factory and wait for the car to come out at the other end. Already, assembling a car today requires the equivalent of less

■ Online Teaching---

Developments in online teaching illustrate possible ways that an intellectual profession, such as that of teacher, can evolve.

One of the primary functions of instructors is to teach in front of a class. The size of this audience is often limited by the size of the lecture halls to a few hundred students, with the result that hundreds of instructors give very similar courses from one university to another. Another function of instructors is to assign students exercises as homework. In this case, an algorithm is sometimes able to assess a student's level better than an instructor by identifying the points that have been understood and those that need to be reviewed, and suggesting tailor-made exercises. Finally, the last function is to grade papers. This work may be replaced by algorithms in various ways. It is more difficult to correct an essay or a paper algorithmically than a multiple-choice exam, but both are possible.

Humans, however, are still better than algorithms in two instances. Instructors are preferable for project-based instruction, which requires understanding the students' objectives in order to help them to achieve them; and more importantly, instructors are better than algorithms in teaching students how to learn. Online instruction is more effective with more advanced university-level students who already know how to organize their learning than with middle-school students who have not yet learned to do so.

Online instruction can replace traditional instruction when the number of teachers is insufficient, for example, in developing countries, or when there is a lack of local expertise in specialized areas. Online instruction involves a radical transformation of teaching methods, and can free instructors from unrewarding tasks such as repeating the same course year after year, allowing them to focus on individual student support. Online instruction is a cost-saving measure. Above all, it is a way of improving the transmission of knowledge from one generation to the next.

than 30 hours of labor, compared with the 40 hours needed in 1980. 3D printers further reduce production time for small parts.

Since the end of the nineteenth century, the use of machines to manufacture objects has transformed our ways of working. For a long time, the occupations that were most changed were exclusively manual, and among those, the least qualified were the most affected. The washing machine, for example, was responsible for the disappearance of the washerwoman. Highly qualified manual professions and the intellectual professions, however, were not greatly affected. A robot might paint a car, but it was difficult to imagine it eloquently posturing in a court of law, performing open-heart surgery, or giving a lecture on general relativity.

We undoubtedly need to reexamine our prejudices. Attorneys, physicians, teachers, and other *intellectual* workers will also soon be partially replaced by algorithms. These professions include a great deal of repetitive work, such as case-law research, prescription writing, and exam corrections. Today we know how to automate some of these tasks and we will know how to automate them even more in ten or twenty years. Algorithms assist humans and already partially replace them, and the number of attorney-, physician-, and professor-hours that we need to accomplish the same tasks will decrease.

Produce More and Work Less?

What happens when productivity increases in this way? There are at least two possible answers to this question. Some, such as Paul Lafargue or Bertrand Russell, saw in this increase of productivity a possibility for man to maintain levels of production while working less and, in the words of Lafargue, "to work only three hours per day [and] to laze around and feast the rest of the day and night." Others, on the contrary, saw a possibility to produce more while working the same amount. When we look at past technical revolutions, it's not at all clear whom history will favor.

For example, in 1870, half of the US active population was employed in agriculture. Today, that number is twenty-five times less. However, the increase in agricultural productivity in the United States did not lead to twenty-five times less work for farmers, nor did it provide a life of leisure and feasting for twenty-four farmers while the twenty-fifth worked. Instead, it had the effect of twenty-four out of twenty-five farmers changing their profession and producing something other than food products, such as locomotives, light bulbs, and medications, that fulfilled other needs and desires. History would seem to favor those who saw, in the increase of productivity, an opportunity to create more while working just as much; and in the end of work, a myth.

This conclusion, however, must be qualified by at least three observations. The first is that in United States, for example, only 150 million out of 328 million people work. Of the rest, 60 million people are younger than fourteen, 50 million are older than sixty-five, 62 million are not in the workforce, including students, and 6 million are unemployed. Compulsory education, an increase in the years of schooling beyond what is required, and retirement allow tens of millions of people to not work. In addition, these 150 million people work relatively little compared with nineteenth-century workers: in the United States, people work an average of 34.5 hours per week. Last, but not least, a non-negligible portion of these practice a profession, such as researcher or instructor, that was once considered a leisure activity. Of course, it is difficult to explain, for example, to an overworked teacher, or to the authors of this book, that they are engaging in leisure activities. The fact remains that the ancient Greek word σχολή, "skhole," from which the word *school* is derived, signifies *leisure*. So, what we have seen in the past is a reduction in the time actually worked, and an even more drastic decrease is likely in the future.

Observing the past thus leads us to differing conclusions. In addition, nothing, other than our intellectual laziness, indicates that our future will be identical to our past. In the past, the increase in productivity in a sector led to the emergence of another sector which fulfilled needs and desires that had been previously unsatisfied or unknown. The increase in agricultural productivity accompanied the emergence of industry; the increase in industrial productivity accompanied the emergence of the service sector. What productive sector may emerge when our need for foodstuffs, manufactured goods, and services will be met by machines? Simplifying somewhat, farmers became workers, workers became taxi drivers, but what will taxi drivers become when cars become self-driving? Will they be idle? What will we find to produce other than foodstuffs, manufactured goods, and services?

A sharp decline in the need for labor is perhaps not a myth. It is a possibility and is undoubtedly already under way. But is this good news?

Freedom from Work

The end of work can be seen as a sort of emancipation. After all, doesn't the Bible present work as a punishment? "By the sweat of your brow you will eat your food until you return to the ground, since from it you were taken; for dust you are and to dust you will return." While waiting for victory over death, couldn't we be satisfied with being rid of work? And which Robinson Crusoe, starving and condemned to fishing twelve hours per day in order to just barely sustain himself, would be disappointed to find, on his island, a horn of plenty that would provide him with meaty fish, steaming roasts, fine wines, and delicious fruits on a daily basis?

However, precisely because we do not live on a deserted island, the end of work is not necessarily good news for everyone. Indeed, as long as tools have been used, the question has arisen of how to distribute the wealth produced between those who provide the work and those who provide the tools, the capital necessary for production; for instance, the fisherman and the owner of the net. In the past, fishing required a net, of course, but above all, work. Building a car required sophisticated factories, but mostly, a substantial amount of work. Workers provided something rare and sought after and that gave them a certain bargaining power with respect to factory owners. The end of work disrupts this distribution of wealth between the providers of capital and the providers of work. Today, factory owners can almost dispense with workers, and they rarely share the profits of increased productivity due to factory automation with the laid-off workers. In the age of algorithms, the pie is larger, but many receive a smaller slice, in relative terms and even in absolute terms.

This is why, since the end of the eighteenth century, workers have sometimes been opposed to mechanization, as during the

Luddite rebellion of 1811–1812. In such cases, mechanization might mean progress for humanity in general, but could just as well be a step backward for workers. When the textile employees smashed the first power looms during this rebellion, it was not because they disliked mechanization, nor that working 18 hours a day on a manual loom was so enjoyable, but because the introduction of these mechanized looms left them unemployed.

It is certainly more difficult today for mail carriers to destroy the servers and dig up the fiber-optic cables that transmit email, but it's not out of the question that, soon, cab drivers and mass transit drivers could destroy the first driverless cars. If tomorrow we discover a horn of plenty that would provide fish for all of humanity, fishermen might attempt to destroy it because humanity must be hungry if the occupation of fisherman is to maintain its usefulness. The destruction of machines is a short-sighted action, but it is a rational reaction.

Let's imagine an extreme case. Assume that we no longer need to work at all to produce food, clothes, means of transportation, and so on, that these objects emerge from a horn of plenty. Could the owners of this horn of plenty keep for themselves the revenue generated by the sale of these objects? The notion of ownership is called into question by even the partial replacement of human workers by machines.

Issues of this type are likely to be at the center of political debate in the twenty-first century, even if, occasionally, attention will be drawn to the *defense* of the interests of one group or another: textile workers, mail carriers, musicians, or cab drivers whose income will be lost to technical progress. In every period of history, technical progress has changed the parameters of political thinking. There would be no Hammurabi without writing, no Martin Luther without the printing press, no Marx without the steam engine. The fundamental political issue facing us is not a reduction in unemployment or the future of mail carriers, but the distribution of the wealth created, without work, by robots and algorithms.

We are already beginning to see these issues arising, at least tenuously, in two recent tweaks to the social contract: universal basic income and the economy of free goods and services. Universal basic income programs have been instituted in different countries. Iran was the first country to install such a program in 2010; since then, a number of other countries have also launched basic income pilot programs. Typically, benefits are very low, and are perceived as temporary assistance toward entering the workforce or returning to employment. However, they are perhaps the beginning of a positive view of unemployment according to which it is not necessary for everyone to work, nor for everyone to work all the time. The miracle cure for unemployment, frantically pursued by successive governments, is perhaps not to put all of the idle people back to work, but to allow them to be happily idle.

The age of algorithms and the emergence of the economy of free also brings into question the notion of property.

9

The End of Property

W here does the apparently paradoxical idea of the economy of free come from?

When a person eats an apple, drives a car, or uses the services of a gardener, he prevents another person from eating the same apple, driving the same car, or using the same services. That makes apples, cars, and gardening services *rival* goods. The more we share a rival good, such as a pie, the smaller each person's slice. In contrast, with a *non-rival* good, the size of each person's share does not change. Non-rival goods have existed for a long time. Listening to the radio, for example, has never prevented another person from doing the same, but radios were historically fairly rare. In the age of algorithms, books, discs, and films, for example, have become digital and can be duplicated at no cost, so they are not rival. In addition, new non-rival goods have appeared such as algorithms and programs.

According to market rules, the price of a good is the cost of an additional unit of the good. This cost is zero for non-rival goods, which results in their being free.

Ownership of Non-rival Goods

The age of algorithms is the age of sharing free digital resources. These resources have already invaded many areas – research, with open-access archives of medical papers such as PubMed Central sponsored by the US National Institutes of Health; education, with online courses, dissemination of knowledge, and free and collaboratively written encyclopedias like Wikipedia; map data, with OpenStreetMap; and government bodies, with the open data movement.

A hard-copy book is partially non-rival. The fact that one person reads it does not prevent another person from also reading it, as long as it is read at a different time, and this partial non-rivalry is utilized by lending libraries which organize the temporary sharing, at almost no cost, of their books. A digital book, however, is reproducible and completely non-rival. The same book can be read by multiple readers without any time constraint.

It is possible to render electronic books artificially rival through the introduction of technically complicated, and not very effective, digital rights management systems. This is sometimes done in order to ensure compensation for the creators and income for the publishers.

If we set aside for a moment the question of author remuneration, which we will come back to, it is indefensible on purely moral grounds to deprive one person of the right to read a book, when the reading of the book by one additional person entails no added cost.

Algorithms and Programs

Like a digital book, an algorithm can be used by an individual without preventing anyone else from using it. An algorithm is a non-rival good, a horn of plenty, and it is certainly unreasonable for its inventor to own it and receive income from it forever. In fact, the law places limits on algorithm ownership. Patent laws limit the duration of ownership of an invention in general. In many countries, patent laws also exclude algorithms from the sphere of patentable inventions.

A program is also a non-rival good, and in the early days of computer science, the few program users exchanged them freely among themselves. In the 1970s, this situation changed because of the competition between software companies. Software previously distributed in source code, readable by a human, began to be distributed in binary code, the result of the compilation of source code which could be interpreted only by a machine. This made any software changes impossible. In reaction to this, at the beginning of the 1980s, the free software movement was born.

In reality, two distinct movements coexist – the free software and the open-source software movements. The free software movement considers that the freedom to use software, to study it, to modify it, and to distribute copies of it, modified or not, are basic liberties. This movement is essentially an ethical one. The open-source software movement puts forth nearly identical goals, but for completely different reasons: to allow, independently of any ethical consideration, the development, by vast communities, of more efficient and more reliable software. Its emphasis is on practical concepts, which is easier for companies to integrate into their way of thinking.

It is fascinating to observe that these movements succeed in offering software licenses, the contracts between the software designer and the software user, that are very similar, starting from motivations that are so different. The most remarkable part of this story is perhaps that they manage to reconcile the ethical and practical considerations so well.

> ■ Richard Stallman
>
> Richard Matthew Stallman (born in 1953, in the United States) is one of the most famous free software activists. He is a talented programmer who has developed many free software programs, particularly editors and compilers.
>
> Stallman created the free software license General Public License (GPL). He is also the inventor of the concept *copyleft*, which uses the principles of copyright law to preserve the right to use, modify, and distribute free software. He is also very active on the digital rights management front.

Thus, many licenses allow authors of software, books, and music to freely authorize certain uses.

Free, but Lucrative

This weakening of the concept of property leads us to one question: How can inventors, computer scientists, musicians, and others make a living if they abandon all ownership of the objects that they produce and all income linked to this ownership? Economic mechanisms have been invented to compensate the authors of goods that are reproducible at no cost.

One example is subscription-based music streaming platforms. Listening to an additional song does not cost more for the user. The platform, however, receives money that it can redistribute to musicians. The motivation of the subscribers is most often to have easy access to a large number of songs and to be able to discover artists at zero cost, while for some, it may also be the desire to financially support artists.

The most interesting examples of new economic models are undoubtedly the mechanisms that support the development of free or open software while at the same time paying the inventors. Some companies develop software and distribute it at no cost for reasons that are anything but altruistic. It may simply be part of a business strategy. A *freemium*, for example, involves first giving away software for free in order to dominate a large market, then selling more advanced versions of the same software. A company can also offer free access to a product it has developed, and then offer services related to the product for a fee, such as training on how to use the product.

A company can also open the software code simply to encourage developers to improve the software by, for example, correcting errors or extending its functionality, which benefits the company. Indeed, many software licenses require users to freely share their added improvements. In this way, many companies become co-developers of large software projects or of a software suite that shares a common standard.

Platforms for cooperative software development play an essential role in making possible the co-development of large-scale software by many developers, often spread out over all continents. This has facilitated the creation of gigantic software programs that no company would ever be able to develop alone. The comparison to the construction of a cathedral is not an exaggeration.

These new economic models are not solely phenomena based on solidarity and libertarian ideals. They are also genuine new patterns of industrial development which may be the harbinger of the decline, if not the disappearance, of the concept of property.

Winner Takes All

However, property has not yet laid down its arms, and, in parallel with the economic sector of free software, cooperative platforms, and public goods, there exists another economic sector where similar conditions have led to very different outcomes: the giant companies of Google, Apple, Facebook, Amazon, Netflix, Airbnb, Tesla, Uber, and Booking.com, among others.

Strangely, the same conditions of non-rivalry, and even anti-rivalry, of goods enabled the emergence of these giant companies. For example, the costs of the company that manages a social network are primarily the cost of software development, and, since software is a non-rival good, the cost is the same whether the number of users is one thousand, one million, or one billion. The costs that are proportional to the number of users, such as the cost of servers or discs, are often negligible. And when we join such a social network, we prefer a network with a billion subscribers over one with a million, because all the friends that we want to communicate with are likely already subscribers.

Social network services are non-rival and even anti-rival. The greater the number who share the pie, the larger the slice of pie for each; the more we use a social network, the greater the size of our own personal network within the social network. Such forces push until there is one single social network, one single online bookstore, one single hotel room reservation platform, and so on. In the age of algorithms, competitive balance is replaced by another law, *winner takes all*, until it is overthrown by another, younger, and more innovative winner.

■ Sergey Brin and Larry Page-------------------------------

The *PageRank* algorithm, created by Sergey Brin and Larry Page, the two founders of Google, was introduced to rank websites in search engine results. Their original public algorithm has been regularly modified to yield today's very secret Google search-ranking algorithm.

When we enter the search words "Elvis Presley," the search engine selects the web pages that contain these two words. There are millions of them, and among them, it selects a small number to show on the first page of results. Google Search, in its early versions, selected the most popular results using a relatively simple algorithm, PageRank, in which each page transfers a bit of its popularity to the pages that it links to making a page even more popular when it is referenced by many popular pages.

This effect applies to companies that produce intangible goods, but it also, paradoxically, applies in part to companies that produce tangible goods. For example, the result of factory automation was that the production cost of an additional car was very low compared with the design cost of a new model.

This natural movement toward monopolies is not unavoidable, but solutions such as the enforcement of antitrust laws or the development of interoperability standards have proven difficult to implement in a global economy.

These two economic models seem very different. On one hand, an economy based on free goods; on the other, immense profits. But are they really incompatible? Wikipedia, for example, is a non-profit company, but it *takes all* in the online encyclopedia market, by essentially imposing itself as the sole encyclopedia. Google makes immense profits, but *Google Search*, *Google Maps*, *YouTube*, and *Gmail* are free services. We will return to this paradox when we discuss personal data and its commercialization in a *two-sided* market. Beyond the intentions of their founders, the only fundamental difference that seems to exist between Booking.com and Wikipedia is that one manages to sell a non-rival good, while the other declines to do so.

— *So, Robot, will algorithms become Caliph instead of the Caliph?*
— *I explained to you that algorithms were created by humans. Humans have to say what they want, and I doubt that you'd want to be controlled by algorithms. Would you like to obey me?*
— *Dream on! You'll continue to serve me. And, when I'm president, will you help me?*
— *That's what we're going to talk about next.*

10

Governing in the Age
of Algorithms

Digital Government

We have all had some experience with the digitization of administrative processes, such as filing taxes online. In certain communities, residents can also, for example, notify authorities of roads in need of repair through a website.

Digital government can simplify public administration and make it more efficient. As in companies, the use of an information system can reduce certain costs, by optimizing the management of a fleet of vehicles. This digitization is accompanied by a reduction in the number of civil servants needed to provide the same public service. This is another example of the replacement of people by machines.

Digital government can also sometimes make public administration more equitable because it is easier for a machine to insist that the same rule be applied to everyone than it is for people, with their habits and their prejudices.

The digitization of public administration does, however, pose some risk to the most vulnerable populations. For example, certain applications for social assistance must be filled out online, yet the potential beneficiaries of this assistance are among the least technologically savvy. The majority of citizens now have access to the internet, but for the minority who do not, this exclusion poses more of a handicap every day. It often leads to cultural, social, and economic marginalization. We must ensure that the digitization of public administration does not aggravate these inequalities.

The right to internet access and the right to the knowledge necessary to use the internet are now basic human rights.

Citizen Participation in Democracy

Computational thinking, as we have seen, describes many human activities as simple exchanges of information. Government at the state and local level is one of the areas in which this view is most accurate. In bakeries, flour is transformed into bread; in factories, crude metal is transformed into cars; but in state and local government, it is only information that is transformed. The mayor of a city may have the impression of planting trees and building daycare centers, but in reality, the gardeners and masons do the work. The mayor can only speak, convince, decide, and mediate. Mayors rarely touch a shovel or a spade. Political institutions are purely informational processes.

Different political systems are merely different ways of organizing the exchange of information. In a dictatorship, information comes down from the dictator to the people. In a direct democracy, information is transmitted from the citizens' assembly to the people in charge of implementing the decisions. In a representative democracy, the flow of information is even more complex. From candidates to citizens, in the form of a platform, from citizens to the agents responsible for vote counting during elections, and, finally, from the elected representatives to the people in charge of implementing the decisions.

In the analysis of these systems, one key issue is the quantity of information exchanged by the agents. Each time we express a choice from among 32 options, we communicate a quantity of information of five bits (as $2^5 = 32$). In California, for instance, where citizens regularly elect national, state, and local representatives and vote on various initiatives, the amount of information they communicate is fewer than 100 bits per year. In representative democracies, if we report the number of bits citizens express in a common unit of measure, the number of bits per second, this is billions of times less than the speed of a home modem.

It is not difficult to understand why our institutions rely on such low-speed communication channels. They were designed in the beginning of the eighteenth century, at a time when elections were organized, at most, about once a year. It is not only because the inventors of the concept of representative government were convinced that people were incapable of governing themselves, but also because communication technologies were not sufficiently developed, that information flow is so slow.

With such a slow speed available to express our desires with respect to diplomacy, the army, the justice system, the police, schools, research, health care, agriculture, lodging, industry, the economy, and so on, we must use a compression algorithm which reduces the size of a message – and often depletes or distorts it in the process – in order to allow for its transmission despite the slow channel. We can sum up our wishes with respect to all of these topics in a short sentence: "On all of these issues, I agree with a particular candidate." This is a classic example of compression with loss. The size of the message is significantly reduced, but there is major loss of content since it is improbable that someone would agree with a candidate on every issue. We compress the message expressing our desires in precisely this way when we vote. The most extreme case of information compression is to sum up our wishes in one bit: *Democrat or Republican.*

The increase in communication speed since the end of the twentieth century has made this way of expressing our desires obsolete. Our two-century-old institutions and the compression algorithms that summarize our desires so simplistically have become outdated. This explains, for example, that new forms of communication have contributed to the development, alongside traditional parties, of political parties focused on specific issues, such as housing rights, migrants' rights, and patients' rights, parties that did not exist in the first half of the twentieth century, with the notable exception of the feminist and ecological parties. Not surprisingly, these parties were the first to rely on the web.

Our institutions, however, continue to ask citizens to compress their desires using the same simplifications, although it is now possible to do things differently. Broadly speaking, in state and local government, we do not take advantage of the possibilities that are available to us in the age of algorithms. This institutional maladjustment to technical progress, in a world that has become much more complex, contributes to the obsolescence of institutions, and to citizens' growing distrust of them.

The institutions we will invent in the twenty-first century will undoubtedly foster increasingly fast information flow. We already see some experiments emerging in this direction. In India, for example, the IPaidABribe project, an initiative of the organization Janaagraha, encourages citizens to fight against corruption by exposing online the bribes that they paid.

Online public consultation during the drafting process of a law, such as for the French Digital Republic Act, are also in line with the trend of allowing citizens to send a greater amount of information to the community. Such a process, one that is consultative and not binding, is insufficient. We can, for example, regret that the French Digital Republic Act that was finally approved does not sufficiently take into account the opinions expressed. In this particular case, many contributions on *commons*, shared cultural and natural resources, were ignored, for example. There was a lot of discussion of the law among citizens, although the text is undoubtedly different than it might have been if it had been written around a table by a few experts before being voted on in the middle of the night.

These types of participatory democracy initiatives are headed in the right direction even though they are still tentative and all too rare. They are facing challenges. First, they should avoid manipulations by special interest groups with disproportionate influence. Most crucially, they must succeed in involving a large enough number of citizens to gain their credibility. Last but not least, the (digital) literacy may be a serious barrier for many citizens. Education is thus essential in this context.

Public Information

The amount of information generated by individuals is a serious issue, and the amount of information received by individuals from public institutions and from other individuals is just as important. Public information, for example, is essential to the well-functioning of representative governments. If members of the public are not properly informed, one can question the meaning of their votes.

Governments now have effective means at their disposal to keep the public informed, although they are a long way from fully exploiting the tools available. For example, in the past, we were used to public data, such as local budgets, being inaccessible, mainly because prior to the age of algorithms, the cost of publishing this information would have been prohibitive. But today, the cost is negligible and we expect this information to be accessible.

The concept of open data is based on the philosophy of free access to information, seen as a public good whose dissemination is in the public interest. This concept of public good is the same that underlies free software and, for example, Wikipedia. In the public sphere, this open data movement has its roots, in the United States, in the Freedom of Information Act of 1966, and has in recent years become quite widespread, notably with the website data.gov. This site provides Americans access to data produced by the federal government; for example, they can follow government expenses in detail.

Information published by newspapers, television, and other media has become much more available and accessible for a longer period of time. The public also receives information from other individuals through social networks, blogs, and forums. Such *horizontal* information has played a critical role in recent political movements, such as the Arab Spring.

This deluge of information, however, complicates the selection of pertinent information by individuals who can also be manipulated by disinformation campaigns.

Companies, Unions, and Associations

While we have emphasized public participation in national and local government, the same issues arise in other institutions, such as unions, associations, and companies.

Less hierarchical organizations have become necessary in these structures and this should help to make them more humane and more effective. They bring new forms of participation, of collaboration in discussion and decision-making, in which trust and consideration are vital.

We are thus faced with an enormous task that includes inventing institutions, companies, and ways of life in society that take into account the potential of communication technologies in the age of algorithms.

— *You know, Robot, I find this world a bit unsettling with these billions of computer programs, and I don't really know what they're up to.*

— *That's why we need to know what they're doing. They absolutely shouldn't do whatever they want.*

— *I propose a law: robots must not commit injustices, they must be nice to me, they must do everything I tell them to do.*

— *And what should they do if you tell them to commit an injustice?*

11

An Algorithm in the Community

The community is usually defined socially as a group of human beings whose life together is made possible by respecting a certain number of rules that define the rights and obligations of each of them. According to this definition, the members of the *community* are women and men. However, a gradual evolution of this concept has led us to consider that groups of human beings, for example, companies, and associations, can also have rights and obligations and, therefore, can also be considered members of the community.

This introduction of hypothetical people greatly simplifies life for us. For example, if Camille, Mark, and Debbie share an apartment and if Camille spends sixty dollars on groceries, it is simpler to say, even if these two formulations are equivalent, that Camille, Mark, and Debbie each owe twenty dollars to the "roommate group," which in turn, owes sixty dollars to Camille. If, for example, Debbie does not pay her debt, it is preferable to view this event as a dispute between Debbie and the roommate group rather than a dispute between Debbie and Camille. When the number of roommates exceeds a few dozen, it becomes simpler for the roommate group, although a hypothetical person, to open a bank account in its name, which assumes that it has rights and obligations with respect to the bank.

In addition to human beings and some groups of human beings, other entities can sometimes be considered members of the community. This is the case for animals, as witnessed by the many instances where charges were brought against them during the Middle Ages, or the fact that French law recognizes them as *sentient beings*. Some modern thinkers propose extending this concept and argue that oceans, rivers, forests, and even robots, software, and algorithms should also be considered members of the community.

Considering a company, an animal, an algorithm, or the software that expresses it, as a member of the community, does not at all mean that the same rights and obligations should be conferred upon it as for a human individual. For example, a court may sentence a human to time in prison, but not a company. Conversely, the court may order the dissolution of a company, but not that of an individual. Considering an algorithm or software as a member of the community is not, therefore, an anthropomorphic identification, but solely an extension of the community to non-human entities. Considering software as a member of the community allows us to see the community as a system where entities, human or not, interact, respecting certain rules. This is a way of making sense of the question of our *coexistence* in the community with software and algorithms, and rules to be established that will ensure that this coexistence is harmonious.

Scapegoats

This coexistence is currently far from peaceful. Algorithms are often perceived as the root of all evil, responsible for the disappearance of jobs, restriction of civil liberties, and the dehumanization of the world, among other things. When the same airplane seat is sold to two passengers, rather than imagining that it might be a human error, or that such errors existed before the use of computers, we think it can only be the fault of the algorithm. These accusations are often aggravated by attitudes firmly anchored in the past, rejection of change, or nostalgia for an idealized past, for example, the idea that digital books distort the pleasure of reading, depriving us of the smell of paper, or that looking up things online dumbs us down, decreasing our taste for learning which had already been thoroughly tarnished by the invention of writing long ago.

Algorithms are chosen, by members of the community, to shoulder the responsibility for errors of which they are not always guilty. They are the scapegoats. In addition to rendering our coexistence with algorithms less harmonious, this designation as scapegoats masks the real issues concerning the place of algorithms in the community. Which decisions should be relegated to algorithms? How do we challenge decisions made by algorithms? Can algorithms be considered morally and legally responsible for their actions?

Decision-making

Like other members of the community, algorithms and computers must make decisions. For example, on roads, fully automated radar evaluates a driver's speed and, depending on the speed observed, decides whether or not to issue a ticket. Nevertheless, we undoubtedly do not wish to delegate all community-related decisions to algorithms. We then have to determine which decisions we want to delegate to them and which decisions we prefer to retain control over.

The justice system provides a classic example of this. Can a court decision be entrusted to an algorithm-judge, just as a speeding ticket can be entrusted to a radar-police officer? We are beginning to encounter such algorithm-judges on the web for small claims dispute resolution online. For example, buyers and sellers on eBay and PayPal can use their *dispute resolution centers* to resolve disputes, and a large number of these disputes are resolved in this way. But can we, in the age of algorithms, go even further and entrust criminal convictions or the parole of convicted criminals to such algorithms?

To answer this question, we first must ask ourselves if we know how to design algorithm-judges that are as effective as human judges. For example, do we know how to design a criminal sentencing algorithm that would make statistically fewer errors than a human judge? Answering this question is not easy, particularly because, in order to evaluate its effectiveness, we would have to compare the relative cost of the unnecessary detention of a potential non-recidivist with that of the release of a recidivist, and be able to evaluate the sincerity of the convicted criminal's repentance, which is perhaps an indicator of a lower risk of recidivism.

That said, merely imagining a non-human judge, rational, impartial, and incorruptible, and then comparing it with human judges, underscores the defects, most likely impossible to correct, of our current system. For example, like all human beings, judges have a metabolism and we know that sentencing judges are significantly less indulgent late in the morning than at the beginning of the afternoon. A study of thousands of cases showed that the proportion of sentence reduction awarded was 20 percent for the last case before the lunch break, and 60 percent for the first case after the same lunch break. We also know that in certain US states, African Americans receive much heavier sentences for similar crimes than other people, whether they are judged by overtly racist juries or simply by juries who, despite their best intentions, have more empathy for people who look like them. We also know that, in many countries, judges are not incorruptible.

In these three cases, we might think that non-human (algorithmic) judges would make better decisions statistically than human judges who could be irrational, partial, and corruptible, as all humans are, to varying degrees. Should we then replace judges by algorithms?

An intermediate solution, between decision-making by an algorithm and by a human being, is hybrid decision-making. In this case, the human being is "advised" by the algorithm. Such a solution, however, has the disadvantage of taking responsibility away from the human being, who could then cite the poor advice of the algorithm in order to justify a bad decision. Likewise, when a decision is entrusted to a group of people, often no single individual is willing to take responsibility. In the example of sentence reduction, a human judge, assisted by an algorithm-judge, would naturally be tempted to not take any risk and to follow the advice of the algorithm when the algorithm advises against sentence reduction. This choice lets the judge avoid responsibility in the event of recidivism, which the algorithm had flagged as likely. The deresponsibilization of human judges is arguably an obstacle to such a hybrid solution.

Conversely, the algorithm is "advised" by humans. It can base its decision only on the data it has been given, and the data come from sources created by humans. How can the algorithm tell whether the data source is irrational or partial?

When all is said and done, should judges be replaced by algorithms? In our current state of knowledge, we are not capable of designing algorithms that possess the necessary empathy to take into account human complexity in each case, or to recognize bias in the data. The issue will definitely come up one day. If algorithm-judges statistically make better decisions than human judges, and we can see why these decisions are better, it will become more difficult to argue that the dehumanization of the justice system is a step backward.

Challenging a Decision

The decision to sentence a person to a prison term is still made by human beings. However, a multitude of small decisions, including issuing a ticket to a driver or approving or refusing a consumer loan, are already made by algorithms. We've all heard of algorithms or computers being used as scapegoats: "Of course you're right, but my hands are tied. It's the computer . . ."

This dictatorship of *computer-assisted mediocrity* should be filed in the same category as other forms of abuse of power in the face of which there is no standard challenge procedure. It is completely normal for an algorithm to make errors. Algorithms are designed by humans who may pass on their own errors and biases. They may not have access to all of the pertinent information, or may not have been designed to take into account a particular situation. It is essential to have access to responsible people who, if they decide that we are right, are able, if necessary, to override the algorithm's decision and impose their own.

Without the possibility of challenging a decision, it is unlikely that algorithm decision-making would constitute progress, and it would certainly not be accepted by the other members of the community. In each case, an authority or a mediator must be able to change the algorithm's decision. And there is nothing that prevents, in certain cases, the mediator from also being an algorithm, better tested and more comprehensive than the one that made the challenged decision.

Aristotle saw the community as composed of *political animals*, united by the choice of a life together. Considering algorithms as political animals, different from us, of course, but still members of the community, leads us to ask new questions regarding the decisions that we would like to delegate to them and the decision-making challenge procedures that we would like to put in place. These questions will help us to better reflect on how to coexist with these algorithms.

12

The Responsibility
of Algorithms

Can an algorithm do harm? Unfortunately, the answer to this question is fairly predictable. Like any tool, an algorithm can be used for better or for worse. For example, if most people receive a pay stub every month produced by an algorithm, it would be very easy to modify the algorithm to add a bonus for certain employees depending on their nationality, skin color, gender, or political opinions. Such discrimination is morally reprehensible whether it is carried out by a human or an algorithm.

The same big data analytics algorithm can make it possible for physicians to personalize treatment and save human lives, and for governments to spy on their citizens in disregard of privacy rights.

When an algorithm does harm, for example, when it acts in a discriminatory way, is it morally liable? This position is difficult to defend, since an algorithm in itself has no intention. In the example of the monthly bonus given to certain employees, the intention to discriminate comes from its designers. Algorithms are not moral actors, and only the people who designed, adapted, configured, chose, and used the algorithm can be held responsible for their actions.

The responsibility for an algorithm's actions belongs to those who design and use it. They must ensure that none of its actions is morally reprehensible and they must assume their share of responsibility, morally and legally, in the event of a dysfunction.

However, as is often the case, while the general ideas are simple, they become more complex when we look at specific cases. One reason is that many algorithms – sometimes thousands – interact, exchange data, reason, suggest, and decide for us. Three examples will serve to illustrate this: self-driving cars, digital personal assistants, and the purchase and sale of financial products.

Who's Driving This Car?

A self-driving car is a car driven by an algorithm. In such a vehicle, sensors analyze the environment, the road, other vehicles, and so on, in real time. The car also interacts with other vehicles and, for example, with traffic lights. An algorithm decides what the car should do – brake, accelerate, turn on the headlights, and so on – and it directs the vehicle to carry out these actions. The passengers can sit back and enjoy the ride.

In such a car, the algorithm is the driver. The algorithm fulfills the role usually assigned to a human being. But let us not be deluded by the deliberately anthropomorphic nature of this example. The responsibility for the actions of this algorithm, as we have said, lies fully with its designers.

While driverless trains and pilotless planes have been widely adopted, driverless cars are slow to arrive on our streets, and there are still many skeptics who think it will never happen. There are certainly a lot of technical problems to solve. There is another reason holding back their rollout. We still do not know how to specify the rules that the driver-algorithm must follow in order to act *correctly*. For example, what should such an algorithm do if it must choose between killing two pedestrians or the sole passenger of the car? Should it be loyal to the car passenger or spare the greatest possible number of human lives?

These issues are very new. Since the development of cars, drivers unfortunately find themselves in these kinds of dilemmas, but as they usually have a few fractions of a second in which to act, they do so without thinking, and do not view their actions in moral or ethical terms. When we take a taxi, we rarely discuss with the driver what he would do in such a situation. But when we design a driver-algorithm, we must answer these types of questions.

Another question slowing the introduction of self-driving cars is that of legal responsibility in the event of an accident. It would be difficult to incriminate the passengers who were watching the world go by. We have seen that blaming the algorithm itself doesn't make much sense. Responsibility must be shared between the natural and legal persons who collectively created the algorithm for the purpose of driving a car. The car manufacturer? The company that developed the algorithm? The company employee who wrote the program? Many others could inherit a share of the blame. And what would happen if the error implicates software components purchased from another company? What if it wasn't a program error, but an incorrect specification of the algorithm? Or the occurrence of a situation that is not even addressed in the specification?

We are advancing slowly on these issues and can already foresee major court cases that will make attorneys and legal experts happy, but we move forward anyway. Some manufacturers, Volvo, for instance, have already announced that they are ready to assume partial responsibility in the event of an accident.

This example shows that the question of the behavior of the algorithm faced with a moral dilemma and the question of legal responsibility in the event of an accident become complicated as soon as we consider a specific case.

That said, there is perhaps a paradox in the fact that we thought – and rightly so, it seems to us – that it is important to answer these questions before allowing these cars to drive in our cities, although today we agree to drive on life-threatening roads with many drivers, some of whom have neither a license nor insurance. We expect a self-driving car to drive, not like the average driver, but better than the best drivers as shown by reactions to the first fatal accident involving a self-driving car. If they are slow to launch, it's because we expect a lot from them. We don't expect them to simply behave in an acceptable manner, we expect perfect behavior, although we don't even always know how to define what that behavior might look like.

Digital Personal Assistants

Digital personal assistants, such as *Siri* or *Google Now*, are another example of the complexity of the questions facing us. These programs are designed to accompany us in our daily life, organize appointments and trips, manage our bank accounts, and so on. Since they answer a real need, they ought to figure prominently in our lives.

In order to work, these programs collect a lot of data about us: data that we deliberately provide that sensors, such as a GPS, produce for us, or even data that our friends provide when they tag us on social media or data retrieved from our suppliers, like the online bookstore that knows all of our literary tastes. Systems collect this data, sometimes without

our being aware, and sometimes without our knowing
how it will be used.

As with self-driving cars, these long-awaited personal assistants are slow to launch and are still quite disappointing.
Why? Until recently, one obstacle to the development of these
systems was that most of the interesting information was
available only in our brains. This argument is no longer relevant. This data is now everywhere, in digital form. Why then,
are these applications so slow in taking hold?

One reason for this delay is, once again, the complexity of
the problem. With the massive availability of data, the problem
is made more complicated. For example, when there are thousands of events that happen around us, our assistant finds it
difficult to select from among these a small number that will be
communicated to us. The assistant must understand the information available, such as images and text in natural language,
which is not easy. Then, the assistant must understand what
interests us. These are tasks that a human assistant can accomplish more or less well. They are extremely complex for a
machine. In addition, information collected by the assistant is
of very poor quality. The information is incomplete, imprecise,
and sometimes incorrect, and making things even more difficult; much of the information consists of opinions and feelings.
Was the restaurant really great, like Camille said? Was Camille
in a really good mood, as Mark said? A personal assistant has to
manage impressions, lies, moods, disagreements, and everyone's love life. All of this adds complexity, which explains
why digital personal assistants are still quite disappointing
and why this topic is still in the research stage.

The greatest obstacle to the development of such an assistant
is undoubtedly the fact that our personal information is dis-
persed across many systems, blogs, social networks, websites,

and so on. These systems store data in different formats, organize it differently, and use different terminologies. In order to have an effective assistant, all of the data would have to be stored in one system. However, we are quite rightly wary of the idea of entrusting all of our data to Google, Facebook, or Apple. We would then be, in a quite worrisome way, entirely at the mercy of the company that we chose. Imagine if our assistant is reluctant to communicate with competitors' software, or if it hides certain information from us because it is not in line with the political or religious positions of the company. Imagine that our assistant distances us from certain friends because they chose a competitor's personal assistant. What if it sells our most personal information to the highest bidder? Such an assistant at the service of a big web company could spell the end of our digital freedom.

How do we define what should be the "moral" or "ethical" behavior of a personal assistant? We dream of a digital assistant who would be of service to us alone, and not to the company that created it. But what does it mean to be "at the service of?"

The Stock Market and Computers

In the world of finance, algorithms, which make decisions on the purchase and sale of financial products, have been the principal actors in markets for a long time. Automated *trading* serves as a good example for a discussion about the question of algorithm *responsibility*.

In 2012, there was a stock market crash. Who can be held responsible for this crash? The algorithms that make the decisions to buy and sell? The computer scientists who designed these algorithms? The people who used them? The algorithms that control the transactions?

We have a tendency to blame the use of algorithms, although the first speculative market crash on record, in 1637, occurred long before automated trading. Attributing blame for stock market crashes to algorithms or to the computer scientists who develop them reveals both a lack of understanding of economic history and a willingness to shirk responsibility. After all, the markets function according to rules that have been defined by human beings, and algorithms are only following these rules.

However, we must recognize that delegating decisions regarding the purchase and sale of securities to algorithms can lead to a weakening of financial markets. This is because algorithms behave differently than the humans for whom the rules were defined. Algorithms make decisions much more quickly, they are extremely uniform in their choices, and they are subject to much less oversight than humans, who are expected to make mistakes.

Rather than unnecessarily accusing algorithms, the solution to this problem is to install new organizational rules on financial markets that take into account the characteristics of algorithms. These new rules must also create an incentive for banks to refocus on their historical organizing role in the savings market rather than counting on the short-term gains that algorithms facilitate. For example, it used to be rare for traders to purchase a financial product in order to resell it less than a second later. While this inertia had a positive effect on markets, we probably should have created a rule that prevents a stock from being sold and purchased thousands of times in one second, for example, by not allowing the resale of a stock within a certain timeframe or by instituting a tax on transactions.

Fake News and Hate Speech

People typically provide content in social networks, blogs, or other forms of digital platform with a lot of enthusiasm. They are happy to participate, argue, and exchange ideas. But, unfortunately, this doesn't always happen in a peaceful and harmonious way. A number of undesirable behaviors are common. Web users are routinely confronted with hate speech and bullying. When we search for information on the web, we often find it but we also run into inaccurate and false information. What is a good medicine for headache? Websites may tell you that it is garlic. Recently, the prevalence of fake news, that is, deliberate disinformation, has reached new dimensions first in United Kingdom with supporters of Brexit, then in United States with those of Donald Trump.

People have insulted and attacked each other in bars or in political meetings since well before the invention of the web. Fake news goes back a long way: the Battle of Kadesh in the thirteenth century BC was portrayed as a great Egyptian victory by Rameses the Great, whereas it was a stalemate. Algorithms allow us to be connected to people within social networks and to insult each other on these same networks. They provide us with more information than ever in human history, but also more errors and lies. Tomorrow, hopefully, algorithms will help us make the web a better place to be, a more reliable source of information.

These examples, through their differences, show us that algorithms can be a force for good as well as bad, and that we should use algorithms only when we are confident that they will perform as intended. We cannot allow self-driving vehicles to turn our roads into a jungle, for digital personal assistants to serve any other interest than our own, or for financial markets to become roller-coasters.

13

Personal Data and Privacy

W hy is the notion of privacy at the core of the issues emerging in the age of algorithms?

We have said that computers allow us to execute, outside our heads, algorithms that we used to run inside our heads. Computers allow us to store, outside our heads, information that we used to learn by heart. The way we access this externalized information is increasingly sophisticated. We use digital calendars, search engines, database management systems, and so on. As with writing, the alphabet, and printing, computer science is part of a vast movement of externalization of our intellectual capacities, particularly our memory.

This is bliss for those who often forget meetings and friends' telephone numbers. However, this externalization also poses a number of problems, in particular because it transforms the very concept of privacy.

Personal Data

We write text: emails, blog entries, and so on. Others write texts that refer to us. We take photos. We listen to music. We watch movies. We buy things. We read web pages and look at our friends' pages on social media. We sometimes comment on them. Our telephone's GPS saves our itineraries. All of this data tells our story.

Computer systems encounter data from multiple sources and make inferences from it. Massive amounts of our data is are collected just about everywhere. Some of the information is correct, some is not. Some is objective fact. Some is completely subjective: someone might find us aggressive, melancholy, in a good mood, and so on. Sometimes we would like to erase information because it reveals things that we would like to keep private. However, secrets are difficult to protect in the age of algorithms, and the right to be forgotten is generally lacking, because we control only a small part of this data. For the most part, we don't even know that it exists, nor do we know what others do with this data.

It is extremely difficult to define *ownership* with respect to this data. Often several people are affected. A photo published on a social network involves the person who took the photo and the people in the photo. The owner of the account for which the photo is published is far from being the sole person concerned. By disclosing personal information, for instance, on social networks, I also disclose information about other people. Companies also produce a lot of information about us. For instance, a Fitbit produces health and fitness information based on my physical activity (heart rate, walking pace, etc.). Does Fitbit own the data it produces? The answer is unclear under current laws.

Rather than defining the concept of ownership of personal data, it is more useful to try to understand which rules could govern the collection, storage, exchange, and use of the data. For this data is of interest to many, and particularly to governments and companies.

Governments

Governments and courts did not wait for the age of algorithms to monitor their subjects and citizens. In the twentieth century, for example, a judge could order a wiretap on a person who was guilty or suspected of an offense or a crime, and governments often dispensed with judges altogether. However, as someone had to spend time listening to these conversations, surveillance was limited.

Thanks to computers and learning algorithms, countries can now run massive surveillance operations of the entire population. The computers of intelligence services run statistical analyses on the mountains of data they collect in order to detect suspicious behavior. The first and last name, address, movement, and personal contacts, along with the movies watched and music listened to, are some of the elements that characterize an individual and indicate to algorithms if this person is suspicious in any way, on purely statistical grounds.

An inoffensive immigrant worker might, by coincidence, live in the same building as an assassin and go on vacation in the same village where an atrocious crime was committed. In isolation, each of these *clues* has no value. Taken together, however, they create a body of data that could lead investigators to consider this person a potential risk to society. What bad luck! The more extensive the surveillance, the greater the number of false positives, that is, the greater the possibility that people will be unjustly deemed suspicious because of an unlucky statistical coincidence, while the number of people correctly under suspicion, limited by the number of criminals, remains comparatively small.

There are many reasons for such widespread surveillance, such as detecting organized crime, terrorism, or human trafficking. Primarily motivated by terrorism, recent laws, such as the *Patriot Act* of 2001 in the United States, and the *Loi relative au renseignement* of 2015 in France, legalize mass surveillance.

It's important to be aware that these laws contribute to the rapid creation of a terrifying *Big Brother*.

The results of the fight against terrorism are, according to specialists, rather disappointing, but that does not prevent intelligence officials from hoping that one day the analysis of the data gathered will produce better outcomes. From a technical point of view, this is probable, unless, of course, the criminals change their behavior or if they start to protect their digital footprint, by, for example, encrypting their communication or using a network such as *Tor* that anonymizes internet connections. The laws that were swiftly passed in the terrifying aftermath of the terrorist attacks led us to restrict our most fundamental rights, in particular, the right to privacy. It is our collective responsibility to question whether this surveillance is well founded, to impose limits, and to place it under the control of an independent judiciary.

Companies

Governments aren't the only ones interested in our data. Corporations, especially the key actors of the web, also understand the value of personal data. Will internet users consent to be continuously monitored and analyzed?

An example illustrating the drawbacks of such monitoring is that of a teenage girl whose father learned of her pregnancy in 2012 through a targeted ad. By analyzing the young woman's purchases, the algorithms used by the company Target correctly determined that she was probably pregnant and sent her discount coupons for baby clothes and cradles. This brutal invasion of family privacy is inexcusable. Sending the advertisement was certainly questionable, and the mere fact that the company was able to infer such personal information is worrisome.

It was shown in the United States that internet users living in low income areas received offers for staplers at higher prices than those in wealthier areas. The company, embarrassed, ended up explaining that the reason was that those internet users lived further away from an office supply store and they were willing to pay more. Is it appropriate for our address to be used to determine the price of an object or service? Imagine we are in a bazaar, haggling with a vendor who has access to all of our personal data. We would be in a rather unfavorable negotiating position.

Do these nuisances have a marginal impact? Because we sign terms of service agreements without even reading them, because we don't take data protection seriously, and so on, the champions of the end of privacy contend that we are ready to consent to our personal data being aired in public. In trying to convince us that younger generations are less sensitive to this issue than older generations, they insinuate that privacy is a problem for the dotards.

The situation is more complicated than that. First of all, young or old, we are not always conscious of the scope of the problem. Second, when we sign those terms of use agreements without even reading them, it's often because we do not have an alternative. We want to access a service and no one else is offering this same service with a data protection guarantee. When we do have the choice, many of us prefer to protect our data. Is it possible to offer the same services to internet users while protecting the privacy of their personal data?

The difficulty is two-fold. First of all, personal data is sometimes useful in improving the quality of certain services. Certain apps tell us, for example, which streets in a city are congested, and they would not be able to do this if they could not locate the cars. Sometimes it is technically possible to develop the same services without collecting personal data, by anonymizing the data collected by such applications, for example, but it is more difficult. Developers are usually content with simple solutions because in order to keep up with the competitive market, new products must be developed very quickly.

Another difficulty is due to the economic models developed by certain large companies that provide, for example, search engines or social networks. They put in place a two-sided market where on one side they offer a *free* service, in exchange for the personal data of their clients, which they then sell on the second side to another category of clients, advertisers, for example.

There are other economic models, like the *personal information management system* (*PIMS*). Users, rather than delegate their services to companies that sell their data, choose to manage their data themselves in a PIMS. If they do not have the desire or the skill to administer computer services, they can delegate this task to a company. Is this just displacing the commodification of data from one company to another? No, because the business model of the service providers is based on the commercialization of their clients' data. A PIMS provider, on the contrary, has a contract with its clients that stipulates that data confidentiality must be protected.

PIMS are still not widely available, but the approach is promising and, most importantly, demonstrates that other ways are possible.

The same techniques that today scatter our data to the four winds can also be used to build very different systems that can respect the confidentiality of private data. Technology does not require data to be public. Only the current economic models and our intellectual laziness lead us to accept it. These models can be changed; new models can emerge if we so choose.

Healthcare Data

Out of all our personal data, some of the most sensitive information relates to healthcare: medical exam results, diagnostics, prescriptions, and so on. This data is complemented by genetic data, since companies like *23andMe* began offering to sequence a large part of our individual genome for a few dollars. Finally, our health also depends on other factors: diet, drug, tobacco and alcohol use, physical activity, exposure to pollution, and so on. All of this is information that we often share willingly, on social media, for example. Taken together, this data largely defines our present and future health.

Some of this data can be collected in electronic medical files, something that we have been expecting for many years. This kind of medical record would have many advantages, for example, for medical research. The analysis of a large number of records could make it possible to identify correlations between certain combinations of drugs and certain pathologies. Most importantly, a medical record of this kind would have many advantages for patients. It could prevent unnecessary exams and perhaps diagnostic errors. Medical records would not be lost when patients change doctors. Over time, it would be possible to create a digital model of each patient in order to personalize treatment.

However, adoption of such electronic medical records systems continues to lag, precisely because this data is sensitive. Should an insurance company or a bank have access to their clients' medical and genomic data or their exercise and sports history? Should an employer have access to employee data?

Medical data is private and, as such, insurance companies, for example, should not be able to access it in order to modify their rates according to the health of their customers, even with their consent. On the other hand, researchers should be able to use it in the interest of medical advances, and healthcare workers as well, in order to improve the quality of care.

Health data should not be locked up, but we must decide who can access such data and, more importantly, what they can do with it. We must also develop the necessary techniques for analyzing massive amounts of data while preserving confidentiality.

Digital Memory

Finally, and this is perhaps the least expected example, how do we preserve our memory? It may seem illogical, but in digitizing our memory, in freeing it from the limits of the human brain, and the limits of analog storage processes, in rendering it infinitely reproducible and potentially immortal, we risk losing it all together.

Observe, for example, the film photos that some of us took in the twentieth century. These photos are often stored in a drawer for decades. Some of the colors are a bit faded, but the photos retain their charm. In a few decades, they presumably will still be there.

Where are the digital photos that we took during our last vacation? Will we still have them in ten years? It is not at all certain. First of all, formats such as magnetic discs and flash drives are less durable than paper. Second, the formats used for these photos tend to become obsolete very quickly. We pile up information willy-nilly, and if there is a computer crash or a change in computer, telephone, or storage system, we "forget" chunks of our memory that are perhaps irreplaceable.

Permanent digital memory is technically possible. Nothing prevents us from saving our photos, regularly updating our discs, regularly reproducing our information, maintaining software for all data formats, or translating our data from obsolete formats to more recent formats. But that has a cost, in particular, a time cost.

We should not be ashamed of our inability to manage our digital memory. Many companies and administrations are no better at it. Solutions for long-term digital archiving are still in the early stages of development. This is why, even after having exchanged information electronically, companies and administrations still use paper archives to maintain records.

That said, this technical problem may mask another one. Back when it was expensive to take a photo, we only took a few dozen photos per year, and even if we kept all of them, it represented a low volume overall. Now that we take several hundred or thousand photos every year, a new problem has emerged. If we want to look at these photos in ten years, without drowning in an ocean of memory, we must learn to select those that we want to keep. Hypermnesia paradoxically renders our memories inaccessible, and we need to learn, with the help of algorithms, to become archivists of our personal digital world.

Collective and Individual Unconscious

Science-fiction writers dreamed of intelligent supercomputers, but they did not foresee the emergence of collective knowledge, constructed by billions of interconnected machines, storing information about us, exchanging this information, and extracting knowledge that tells our story – everything we ever wanted to know about each one of us, and more.

Information systems, by interacting and analyzing all of the data related to an individual, can discover aspects of the personality of this individual that the person would like to hide, or even disregard completely. Big data analytical algorithms have, in a way, direct access to our unconscious. Like psychoanalysts, they are less interested in the logic of our discourse than in the words that we use, their associations and correlations, and so on. Algorithms predict what we will buy without us even being conscious of it.

Our unconscious today is within reach of algorithms, like a collective unconscious waiting to be explored.

We are discovering the risks to our personal data from government and corporate attacks and from the effect of time. In any case, solutions do exist and we should implement them on an individual as well as collective level. With respect to governments, the solutions to improve protections for private data are primarily a matter of policy. Unsurprisingly, with respect to companies, the solutions are primarily economic. With respect to time, the solutions are first and foremost personal. We are the ones who must decide what we want to remember.

General Data Protection Regulation

Since the publication of this book in French, huge progress on the issue of protection of digital personal data in Europe was made in 2016 with the approval by the European Parliament of the General Data Protection Regulation (GDPR). Personal data is defined in very general terms: "personal data is any information relating to an individual, whether it relates to his or her

---

■ Cynthia Dwork--

Cynthia Dwork is an American computer scientist. She pioneered research on privacy in data management systems. In particular, she proposed ways of blurring databases to preserve privacy, similar to what is done for photos. One of her major contributions is the definition of *differential* privacy, a statistical technique that enables the maximization of the accuracy of query answers, while minimizing the privacy impact on individuals with information in the database.

---

private, professional or public life." It includes all data that can be identified with a person. The core principal is that individuals should have control over their personal data. For instance, they have the right to access their personal data gathered by internet companies, and to be informed about how this data has been processed. They also have the right to request the erasure of personal data under certain conditions. A number of countries, such as Japan, are now considering adopting similar regulations. Even when a company is not physically present in the EU, if it collects personal data relating to EU nationals, for example, through a website, it is subject to all the obligations defined by the GDPR.

14

Fairness, Transparency, and Diversity

We have certain expectations of the algorithms we use. For example, we would like them to be *fair*. These properties are essential for the peaceful coexistence of humans and algorithms, and for establishing a climate of trust in the community. They are even more critical when these algorithms exercise a certain power, such as when an algorithm makes the decision to approve or refuse a bank loan. What exactly are these expectations?

Fairness

In order for a decision concerning an individual to be fair, it must deliberately ignore certain information, such as the gender or ethnic origin of the individual. This is what the allegory of blindfolded Justice symbolizes.

It is often difficult to know if human beings make fair decisions or not. For example, how can we be sure that the maître d' of a top restaurant does not give a better table to patrons who are more famous, better dressed, or more beautiful? Likewise, are the authors of this book absolutely certain that they have never unconsciously favored one student over another during an oral exam because of the way they were dressed?

Replacing a restaurant maître d' or an examiner of a competitive examination by an algorithm may contribute to increased fairness since, when we express this algorithm by a program, everything must be explicit. It is possible, of course, to design an algorithm that, when we reserve a table on a website, begins by searching if our first name is on one list: Jorge, Fang, Fatima, Moshe, and so on, or on another: Michael, Emily, Nancy Peter, and so on, and selects one table or another according to the result of this search. However, in contrast to the unfathomable motivations of the maître d', making explicit this type of criterion for assigning a table would be rather negative publicity for the restaurant. Such discrimination, always immoral, is, furthermore, quite illegal, when, for example, a bank offers different interest rates to members of an ethnic minority.

Certain biases are easy to detect. By analyzing the program that implements it, we can fairly quickly identify if the algorithm that decides whether a bank loan is approved or refused bases its decisions on the value of the attribute *Religion*, in a database. Others are more difficult to detect, such as when a certain algorithm analyzes a data set that includes the first names of the applicants, their country of birth, their food habits, and so on, then calculates a variable X244 and uses it to guide its decision, and this variable is "coincidentally" strongly correlated to the applicants' religion. Last but not least, the algorithm may be unbiased but base its decisions on biased data sets. This may be the case for machine learning algorithms that are trained on biased human data and that zealously reproduce the biases.

This is why we must be doubly vigilant when analyzing these algorithms.

Transparency

It may be easier to prove unfair intention in an algorithm than in a maître d', because everything is explicit in the expression of an algorithm. However, in order to prove that an algorithm is biased, we need to know how it works. This brings us to the issue of algorithmic transparency. To shed some light on this question, we need to begin by distinguishing several types of algorithms. Some algorithms, such as the symbolic or non-symbolic algorithm that allows us to distinguish between a dog and a cat, are employed by our brain without us knowing how they work. Specifying image recognition algorithms and observing the functioning of our brain helps us, little by little, to understand them better. The fact that algorithms must be explicitly specified can be seen as a factor of transparency.

In contrast, other algorithms, such as addition and multiplication algorithms, have been used for thousands of years by human beings. When we multiply by hand, we know exactly how this algorithm arrives at the answer, because we calculated it ourselves, step by step. By having computers run the algorithms, we have lost some of this transparency. It is still possible to execute a simple algorithm step by step and to explain the calculations performed at each step. This is what the *OpenFisca* platform does, with algorithms that calculate taxes and social benefits. However, when a computer runs a million operations to reach a result, even if we know what the operations are, and even if we could, in theory, calculate each one by hand, we might be surprised by the result. This is often the case with big data analytics algorithms. It is difficult to explain the millions of operations that led to the decision that a street should be made one-way, based on the analysis of terabytes of data, gathered by the equipment services.

The complexity of the calculations that can be performed by a computer, as well as the amount and type of data these calculations are performed on, can be seen as factors of opacity. Finally, an algorithm designer can decide to share it with users or to keep it secret. If a restaurant decides, for example, to keep secret the algorithm it uses on its website to assign tables, the specification of the algorithm is no longer a factor of transparency.

It is difficult to remedy the opacity that is due to the complexity of algorithms. However, it is easy to require that algorithms that make decisions affecting us be made public.

To draw a parallel, data analysis has been part of the scientific method for a long time, and researchers recognize the importance of using transparent data and data analysis methods if they want their results to be accepted by the scientific community. Similarly, for the algorithms that make decisions affecting us, this transparency contributes to a climate of trust and makes us more comfortable with the results of algorithms.

Unfortunately, we frequently experience failures of algorithmic transparency. For instance, the *Investigatory Powers Act 2016* in United Kingdom or the *Loi relative au renseignement* in France provide intelligence services with enormous means of citizen surveillance. Governments have access to masses of data that they can process algorithmically in a totally opaque manner. The secrecy around the ranking algorithms of web search engines allows the introduction of biases in favor of the services of the companies providing these engines. Lack of transparency in a number of algorithmic decisions, from e-commerce pricing to judicial sentencing, has been shown to reinforce biases based, for instance, on race or gender.

Yet transparency is a relatively easy objective to achieve. In some cases, it would be enough to publish the algorithm.

Even if the program is complex, it could be analyzed by experts and tested on independent data in order to clarify how it works. When the decisions are based on massive volumes of data or on the training of an algorithm on large data sets, this becomes more complicated. But one should be able to explain the algorithm decisions when they have important impact on people's lives.

We are much more demanding of transparency in our relations with machines than in our relations with humans. When, for many years, judges alone were responsible for making decisions to grant or deny parole, their performance evaluation was rarely seen as an issue and the fairness of their decisions was not really measured. However, when algorithms are used to make decisions or simply to assist in decision-making, the biases of these algorithms are very appropriately questioned and scrutinized.

We are more demanding in part because of our suspicion of machines. But the true reason is that this transparency is easier to achieve with an algorithm than with a human being. The age of algorithms provides us the opportunity to bring more transparency into the functioning of the community. We should seize this opportunity.

Diversity

The simpler they are, the more algorithms have a propensity for regularity and uniformity.

In the case of big data analytics, algorithms have a natural tendency to make the most popular choices each time. For example, movie recommendation algorithms are based in part on the number of people who have seen a film. The more people have seen it, the more it is recommended, and the more it is recommended, the more people will see it. With this kind of algorithm, everyone might see the same movie without even knowing that other movies exist, and in doing so, kill off any cinematographic diversity and any element of surprise. This is true even if at the beginning only a few more people saw the "most popular" movie. Recommendation algorithms like that of Netflix are more complex, but they only refine this notion of popularity. They are based on the opinions of people like ourselves. The algorithm recommends films that people with similar tastes to us have enjoyed. The risk of being surprised by a film or a book is even less likely.

However, it does seem important, and even fair, to not neglect the less popular selections. Some views that in the beginning were very much in the minority, such as heliocentrism (worldwide), or the abolition of the death penalty (in Europe and Latin America, but not United States), eventually became the dominant views.

On dating sites, a small number of people can also dominate the rankings and have a considerable, and perhaps unfair, advantage. Likewise, on crowdfunding platforms, a small number of projects can monopolize all of the attention, which can limit the "productivity" of these systems.

Solutions are beginning to emerge, such as introducing randomness, as in the ants' search algorithm for finding food (see Chapter 2), and grouping responses into themes.

Trust

The community cannot function if its members do not have a minimum of trust in each other. If we did not have confidence in banks, we would not deposit our money with them. If we did not have confidence in other drivers, we would not drive cars.

In the same way, it is essential that we have confidence in the algorithms we interact with every day in the community.

The equity and transparency of algorithms, the fact that they are conscious of diversity, but also their reliability and their safety, are properties that are essential for building this trust. Dialogue between different members of the community is another essential factor in building a climate of trust. Algorithm users must, for example, better organize to engage in dialogue with companies, to identify best practices, and prevent unfair or opaque practices. The Instagram controversy of 2012 illustrates their power. The company had changed its privacy policy without clearly informing its more than 100 million users. An outcry among users prompted Instagram to reverse the changes.

Obviously, governments also have a responsibility to participate in defining the broad principles and general guidelines for establishing an environment where machines and humans can coexist in a climate of trust. Some governments, for example, the European Union, are attempting to do this.

Understanding Each Other Better

One final factor for improving trust within the community is for its members to get to know each other. Humans and algorithms have a long way to go before they understand each other.

Algorithms still provide interfaces that are often too complicated, too rigid, and unusable. This shows their ignorance of the expectations of the humans they are supposed to serve. The good news is that these interfaces are improving. Some try, for instance, to analyze user emotions and to adapt themselves accordingly.

But it takes two to understand each other. The situation of humans and algorithms is admittedly not symmetrical. Algorithms are the ones that should adapt themselves to humans, but it would also be useful for humans to understand a bit better what algorithms do, for example, what free software is or what learning algorithms do.

These principles of fairness, transparency, accessibility, and respect for diversity are not new. For centuries, democracies have struggled to guarantee these principles for their citizens. Algorithms can allow us to further develop them. Algorithms can be more fair than humans, they can bring more transparency to administrative processes, and they can offer more personalized service, taking into account the diversity of the members of the community. But they can also do exactly the opposite.

The arrival of the age of algorithms allows us to choose from a greater diversity of social models. But this also comes with increased responsibility. Algorithms are not intrinsically fair or transparent. Nor are they unfair or opaque. They are exactly as we make them. It is up to us to choose how we want to live, although imposing our choices will require a lot of effort in a world dominated by giant corporations.

— *Do you know what my friends call you? Geek Robot, because you bore us with your algorithms.*
— *I can give you a nickname, too. I'm going to call you Ms. Green. Why?*
— *Because you're so into ecology.*
— *Is there a love or a hate relationship between ecology and computer science?*
— *A little of both, with some big fights.*
— *Go on, tell me about it!*

15

Computer Science and Ecology

Algorithms transform the relationship between human beings and nature, and in doing so, transform nature itself. This leads us to examine the relationship between the digital revolution and another transformative factor in our world today: the ecological transition.

Since these two transformations are occurring in the same era, our own, we should examine the interaction between them. The analysis of this interaction is made difficult by the fact that there is no more unanimity in computational thinking than there is in ecological thinking. In trying to identify what unites or opposes computer science and ecology, we often run the risk of simply identifying what unites or opposes certain computer scientists and certain ecologists. It is nevertheless possible to try to identify some overall trends that transcend differences within one movement and the other.

Algorithms and Global Warming

Although environmentalism has been around, in more or less the same form, since the end of the 1960s, one of its defining areas of engagement since the end of the 1980s has been in the fight against global warming. The global warming hypothesis owes much to a revolution in science that occurred with the earliest computers – the development of large-scale algorithmic models. Climate models led us to conclude that the atmosphere and the oceans would warm in the future. The experts of the Intergovernmental Panel on Climate Change, created in 1988 "to provide the world with a clear scientific view on the current state of knowledge in climate change and its potential environmental and socio-economic impacts," based their work on such models.

In addition to predicting climate change, if we maintain the same patterns of development, these models can also be used to evaluate the effectiveness of the strategies devised to mitigate warming of the atmosphere and the oceans. It is enough, for example, to change one parameter in an algorithmic model, such as carbon dioxide or sulfur dioxide emissions, to evaluate the impact on atmospheric or ocean temperature of reducing or increasing these emissions. In this way, computer science has become an indispensable tool for studying climate change.

Algorithms and Complex Systems

Computer science is also an indispensable tool for managing complex energy systems. To produce electricity in the twentieth century, large units such as nuclear power plants or dams were constructed, and then the electricity produced was distributed over a large area. The organization of such a system was relatively simple.

Today, the more sustainable option is to find a more local solution. Such solutions, however, are much more complex. The goal is to produce electricity locally and distribute it locally, which means minimizing the movement of the electricity produced. This requires cooperation between numerous, and very different objects – solar panels, wind turbines, thermal power stations – that must adapt rapidly and continuously to variations in demand, and manage multiple interactions and constraints. All of this can be accomplished only by using algorithms.

For example, a *smart* electricity grid can make it possible for a large number of consumers and providers to exchange electricity, similar to the way in which computer networks exchange data. Such a network must continuously adapt production to demand. This can only work with sophisticated optimization algorithms. We could perhaps run a nuclear power plant without a computer, but not a smart electricity grid.

While ecology encourages decentralizing electricity production, it also supports decentralization in other areas, such as agricultural production, giving rise to local agriculture. This leads once again to complex production and distribution systems, to economic models that can be successfully deployed only with the help of optimization algorithms, management systems for flow, social networks, and web services.

Computer Science, Consumer of Electricity

This brings us to a question that divides rather than unites computer science and ecology: electricity consumption by computers.

The first computers, such as ENIAC, consumed as much electricity as a small city. Today's smartphones are more powerful than ENIAC, but they consume almost nothing. Computers use less and less electricity, but there are more and more of them so that, taken together, including the billions of smartphones, tablets, and all of the data center computers, they are major energy consumers. This electrical consumption is responsible for 2 percent of carbon dioxide emissions in the atmosphere. These emissions are significantly lower than urban heating and car emissions, but they are already comparable to carbon dioxide emissions due to air travel. This warrants reflection on ways to reduce electricity consumption.

Some have suggested, for example, that we refrain from sending unimportant email or that we avoid sending large attachments. Such savings are marginal. Soon, 80 percent of world traffic on the internet will consist of videos. Email, with or without attachments, represents a fraction of data traffic and, therefore, of electricity consumption. However, optimization of video traffic could have a non-negligible impact. Most often, the streaming videos that we watch are housed on a server very far from us, which makes transferring them to us costly in terms of electricity. If we can find the same video on a server closer to us, for example, on the server of a neighbor who has recently watched it, the power required to get it to its destination would be much less. Use of *peer-to-peer streaming* is still fairly rare. It could, however, be a source of significant savings.

Another idea being studied is to recover the heat produced by computers. Like an electric radiator, a computer converts electrical energy into thermal energy, but unlike a radiator, whose primary purpose is the production of thermal energy, in the case of the computer, this is a secondary effect. It is irreversible; we cannot completely reconvert the thermal energy into electrical energy. However, we can take advantage of the thermal power itself. This is actually what happens when we use a computer at home in winter. In addition to calculations, the computer also contributes to heating the house and we can turn the heater down a notch, saving exactly the electricity used by the computer.

However, this is not what happens in a *data center* where the thermal energy emitted by the computers is released into the atmosphere through the ventilation system. Hence the idea of using this heat where we need it, by heating our homes, for example. Such solutions are not yet widespread, but we can imagine that in the future, computers could replace our electric radiators that simply convert electrical power into thermal power without even using it to carry out calculations.

In addition to electricity, computers require other resources. Producing their batteries and screens requires, for example, the use of *rare earth elements* such as lanthanum. Contrary to what their name suggests, these metals are fairly abundant in Earth's crust, but their extraction is challenging and very toxic for the populations living near the mines. In some countries, they are extracted in appalling sanitary conditions.

At the other end, since computers, telephones, and tablets have a fairly short lifespan, they are quickly disposed of, and only a small fraction of these devices is currently being recycled.

Computer science is now so much a part of our lives that it has become necessary to take into account the different aspects of its development – the electricity consumed by running computers, the materials used to make them, and their disposal once they are no longer being used. One solution would be to produce less fragile and more sustainable objects.

Values

Many computer scientists and ecologists share a certain number of values. For example, they are in agreement that humanity, by its actions, can transform the world. The *Silicon Valley* series' somewhat ironic slogan, "To make the world a better place," could also be an environmental slogan. The solidarity and sharing of knowledge that are at the heart of the free software and open data movements are also at the heart of certain environmental movements.

However, computer scientists and ecologists can be in disagreement over what constitutes progress. Computational thinking is by nature quite open to change, and sometimes neglects to question whether change is really progress. In contrast, ecological thinking is sometimes conservative, such as when it argues for the unchanging and immutable protection of nature.

Computer science and ecological evolutions converge on several points, but there are also points of friction. They are both powerful societal factors of transformation and their interactions shape in part our future.

- *Why do you always say I bore you with my algorithms?*
- *I'm just kidding. I'd rather go play with my friends than go to my computer science class.*
- *Yet I can't tear you away from your screen when you're writing programs.*
- *You're right, I love that! But, what's actually the point of learning about computer science?*

16

Computer Science Education

In many countries, governments are now conscious of the importance, in the age of algorithms, of computer science education. In the United Kingdom, for example, the Royal Society published a report in 2012, "Shutdown or Restart: The Way Forward for Computing in UK Schools," recommending the introduction of computer science education in schools. At about the same time, Google chairman Eric Schmidt's devastating critique attracted a lot of attention: "I was flabbergasted to learn that today computer science isn't even taught as standard in UK school. Your IT curriculum focuses on teaching how to use software, but gives no insight into how it's made." As a result, the United Kingdom engaged in a complete reconstruction of its computer science educational system. In the United States, an "advanced placement" course called AP Computer Science was introduced in 1984 as a specialized high school subject. But the education system is quite fragmented and schools are not required to offer it. Barack Obama declared in 2016, "In the new economy, computer science isn't an optional skill. It's a basic skill, right along with the three R's." In 2018, only about 135,000 out of the 15 million high school students in the United States were enrolled in the course.

Computer science education was briefly introduced in France in the 1970s. It was only in 2012 that it reappeared in the high school curriculum as a tentative specialized subject in the last year of high school for students in the science stream. It has since spread to the primary and middle school levels. Much remains to be done, particularly in recruiting enough qualified teachers.

There are at least two reasons for studying computer science. First, to help live in our world where algorithms are everywhere, and second, to work in the field.

These two motives are not in contradiction. Understanding mobile apps and how they are developed, for example, is useful both on a professional and on a personal level. The same hairdresser who develops, or hires someone to develop, an appointment app for clients probably also uses an app to plan family vacations. Naturally, the relative importance of these two motives varies according to the age of the students. The primary school's mandate leans more toward the development of young citizens. At the high school level, however, students are beginning to prepare for their professional future.

Living in the Age of Algorithms

One reason for studying computer science is to prepare students for life in a world where algorithms are everywhere. In order to do so, they must learn how this world works. Schools today explain a great deal more about how the twentieth-century world worked than about how the twenty-first century world works. For example, electromagnetism helps us understand the landline telephone. But today's smartphone, with its millions of lines of code, manipulates digital information, and understanding it requires knowledge of the algorithms that make it work.

We have seen that computer science transformed the concepts of work, ownership, government, responsibility and private life, and so on. Today it is impossible to understand our world without some grasp of computer science. This is why it has become necessary to also teach computer science alongside subjects like physics and biology.

Working in the Age of Algorithms

In high school, students begin preparing for a career. Some of them will be computer scientists. The IT sector suffers from a chronic problem of negative unemployment; there are more job opportunities than people to fill them. We therefore need to train more young people for IT jobs. From information system manager to website designer and software developer, these jobs depend on a very broad set of skills and can be filled by students with a wide variety of talents: mathematical, organizational, artistic, and so forth. New careers are constantly appearing. For example, just a few years ago, the profession of *data scientist* did not exist.

This profession is a good example of the multidisciplinary nature of computer science. A *data scientist*, whose work consists of analyzing massive amounts of data, must be skilled in computer science, but also in statistics and often in the field in which the data is being analyzed. Data scientists specializing in data journalism must also learn about the journalistic profession. Developing skills in three such different areas requires long years of study and continued education throughout one's life.

The basics of computer science are also useful outside the IT professions since innovation enabled by computer science constitutes one of the main factors of corporate competitiveness. This holds, for example, in the automotive industry, where software development represents an important part of the cost of new vehicles, but also in the retail industry, which has seen the emergence of web purchases; in education, transformed by online courses; in agriculture with tractors driven by GPS; and so on.

Likewise, in research, plasma physicists often spend most of their time developing simulation software. They are, of course, physicists first and foremost, but they are now also part computer scientists. Similarly, it is not possible today to explain biology, economics, or climatology without talking about algorithms.

Are there professions in which computer science doesn't play a role? Perhaps taxi drivers thought they could practice their profession without an understanding of computer science. But in just thirty years, they have lived through three revolutions. First came the GPS, which made it possible for taxi companies to hire drivers who didn't need to know where the Brooklyn Bridge is in New York or the Champs-Élysées in Paris, because the GPS would guide them. Then, online reservation apps allowed them to exchange information with their clients, dispensing with the need for the light on the roof, which brought about the emergence of unlicensed taxis, or private vehicles with drivers. Finally, self-driving vehicles are coming and will undoubtedly change the profession for good. Professions evolve rapidly in the age of algorithms and everyone needs to understand some computer science in order to anticipate these changes and to prepare for them, rather than to simply submit to them.

What Should Be Taught?

Defining the content of a new course of study is not an easy task: What is the essential knowledge and what are the techniques that must be mastered?

In a rapidly changing field like computer science it is tempting to always want to be on the cutting edge, always teaching the latest innovation. That is the surest way to always fall behind. That is why, on the contrary, we should focus on perennial knowledge. Instead of teaching the latest programming language, we should teach the principles of programming, the fundamental structures common to all languages, and the reason for the plurality of languages. Of course, one or more languages are needed in order to put this knowledge to use, but even the disappearance of these languages would not be of great importance because the students will have learned how to learn other languages.

When the pioneers began teaching computer science at the university at the end of the 1950s, they were finding their way and experimenting. Today, although we can always improve our thinking, we have enough perspective to agree on the content of a computer science course. The fundamental knowledge base is organized around four main concepts: algorithm, machine, language, and information. Students should also learn the rudiments of computational thinking (see Chapter 6).

An important step in learning about computer science is to apply that knowledge by learning how to program. In any case, this study should not become an end in itself. The objective of this teaching is not to train expert programmers.

Students also need to understand how computer science has transformed companies by structuring them around information systems. They should also understand how it transformed other areas of knowledge, such as biology. In the beginning, computer science was used as a tool for performing computations, as in gene sequencing. Then, computational thinking became more widespread in biology, and computer science was used to describe and simulate, for example, cell function.

This pattern is seen in many other disciplines: statistics, physics, social sciences, and the humanities. The language of algorithms has become a lingua franca uniting the sciences.

How to Teach It?

Computer science is both science and technology, and both aspects are essential for computer science education. Trying to teach computer science at the blackboard as math is traditionally taught can lead to many students becoming disenchanted with the subject. In computer science, the best results are obtained though project-based learning, mostly carried out in teams.

Let's visit a middle-school computer science class. The classroom resembles an open space work environment. The students are working in small groups trying to accomplish a goal, for example, studying the growth of their town throughout history. The data for this study is available on the web. The students first tried using some graphic software that didn't do exactly what they wanted, so they decided to write their own program to illustrate their data graphically. The instructor then taught them an algorithm to do this. The students analyze problems, propose solutions, and test them. In so doing, they discover the basics of software design methods. They learn from their interactions with the instructors, with other students, and also from their mistakes. Their instructors almost have to kick them out at the end of class. They always want to stay to test one last idea.

We used a historical geography project as an example. We could have chosen one related to physics, biology, literature, economics, and so on. Teaching computer science is also an opportunity to open up the walls between disciplines.

Inclusion

Most school systems were founded on the idea of equality, but many observers are alarmed by the fact that they are producing more and more inequalities. Students are often abandoned along the way, feel disconnected from school, and are at risk of dropping out. Wouldn't adding even more subjects to a curriculum that is already overloaded lead to even more students dropping out? We don't think so, for at least three reasons.

First of all, computer science appeals to many at-risk students who find that these courses make school more appealing. Teamwork, a concrete objective to reach, and the opportunity to learn from mistakes provide them at least one subject they can do well in, and sometimes gives them confidence that they could also succeed in others.

Second, understanding computer science demystifies certain digital tools, which allows these students to catch up in other core subjects. For example, in rich digital environments, students learn reading, writing, and computation. Many students are more engaged when they use computers and show at least partial improvement in writing performance, vocabulary, and spelling.

Finally, computer science instruction prevents computer science objects and knowledge from becoming social markers. Children of privileged environments have access to better computers, tablets, phones, and, especially, computer science instruction outside school. The other students are even more excluded from the world of algorithms. Computer science instruction at school would prevent this exclusion.

— *Robot, are we so different from each other? I can put on prosthetic legs and run as fast as the world's fastest blade runner, Blake Leeper, and soon, with a memory extension of a few terabytes, and I won't have to study anymore.*
— *But you would still be a person and I, a robot.*
— *Are you more intelligent than me?*
— *Very intelligent humans have tried to define intelligence, but they haven't really succeeded. I don't know if I'm intelligent, but I am an expert swindler. On the phone, I can pass as you and your friends wouldn't notice a thing.*
— *Robot, do you love me?*
— *Yes, if it pleases you.*
— *Do you love me for real?*
— *Not for real, if it scares you. Let's say, I love you, for pretend.*

17

The Augmented Human

W hat could we still say was unique about us in the twentieth century?

Of course, we know that Earth is not at the center of the
Universe. And we also know that we are eukaryotes, of
the animal kingdom, the class of mammals and the order
of primates. We further distinguish ourselves by several qual-
ities. We have the gift of speech; from generation to generation
we transmit cultures that distinguish us from each other; we
are self-aware; we exchange goods; we are capable of empathy;
and so on. Our myths and fables remind us of these distinc-
tions when they play on the incongruity of a grasshopper and
an ant conversing like humans, and when a wooden puppet
becomes a boy.

Humanism, this idea of the uniqueness of man in the world,
is, paradoxically, being questioned on a scientific and philo-
sophic level at the same time that its many positive effects in
the moral sphere, such as respect for human life, are being
celebrated. Two reasons lead us, in fact, to question the uniqueness of man. The first comes from the study of animal behavior. It turns out that self-awareness, language, the transmission
of culture, and so on, which we believed to be the sole province
of humankind, is actually present to varying degrees in the
animal kingdom.

The second is that we lose some of this uniqueness each
time we design an algorithm capable of simulating a faculty

that, up to that point, we believed to be exclusively human. Playing chess, for example, was for a long time considered the perfect example of a typically human ability. We have never managed to teach this game to a bonobo or a wooden puppet. The chess-playing automaton built at the end of the eighteenth century by Johann Wolfgang von Kempelen was a fake. However, since world champion Garry Kasparov's loss in 1997 to the IBM computer Deep Blue, no one has dared to claim that a computer cannot play chess.

This questioning of humanism has led to the development of currents of thought that propose, for example, augmenting humans through hybridization with machines, or maintaining that computers have, or will soon have, true intelligence and real feelings. More than a matter of being true or false, these theories have the benefit of making us take a fresh look at an old question: What is this thing we call *humanity*?

Our Augmented Faculties

A calculator can multiply, not as well as a human, but better – that is, faster while making fewer errors. So why don't we enhance our faculties to carry out multiplication, for example, by hybridizing ourselves with machines? We can think of several ways to do it. We could transplant an electrical circuit in our skull, or, less ambitiously, we could insert a cable into our skull to which we could connect an electrical circuit that would remain outside our body. These two solutions are geometrically different, but functionally identical.

The second solution has the benefit of showing us that we are already cyborgs. There are already cables coming out of our skulls – our optic nerves. These nerves connect seamlessly to computers using an interface made of a screen and two eyes.

Our motor nerves also connect seamlessly to computers using two hands and a keyboard.

As soon as we move beyond the disturbing idea of connecting a computer's optic cable directly to our optic nerves, short-circuiting the screen and the eyes, the banality of this hybridization idea becomes rapidly apparent. Ever since we began making tools, we have been augmented by them. Hammers augment the strength of our arms; books and libraries augment our memories; hearing aids and cochlear implants augment our hearing; and so on. It's not surprising that, in June 2018, the sprinter Blake Leeper, double amputee, ran with prosthetics, becoming the world's fastest blade runner, as fast as the best athletes. We have always known how to surpass our abilities through the use of tools. The only true question is, in the interest of athletic equity, to know if, in this particular case, the absence of prosthetics doesn't handicap the other athletes.

Another Species?

Once augmented, are we still human? Or do the cyborgs we've become constitute another species, transhumans, with whom humans are in competition in a process of natural selection?

If this is the case, transhumans would be the first species made by a previous species and not the product of differentiation. If this is the case, and if transhumans have been constructed to be better adapted for survival in their environment, then we can also predict that humans will be at a disadvantage in the process of natural selection and that they are an endangered species.

Again, once we get passed this disturbing way of asking the question, its banality is obvious. The notion of species is one of the poorest defined in biology, to the point that we can ask ourselves if Neolithic farmers belonged to the same species as Paleolithic hunter-gatherers. If we decide that it is not the case, we can then say that a new species appeared in the Neolithic and that this species supplanted the hunter-gatherer species which is now extinct, with the exception of a few specimens hidden away in the depths of the Amazon.

Does this way of describing the Neolithic revolution put it in a new light? We doubt it.

We think it is more pertinent to assume that this faculty of augmentation, the technique, is part of our humanity. Some humanists even thought for a time that it was a characteristic of our humanity. We are never more human than when we replace an amputated arm with a prosthesis driven by our brain.

Customized Humans?

Also more relevant is the question of the limits that we should impose on ourselves, for ethical reasons, in this process of human augmentation.

For example, we can worry about the possibility of augmenting our children using an algorithm for genomic selection from conception. If we allow wealthy parents to conceive custom-made children – it would be the first eugenics program in history in the etymological sense of the word εὖ "good" and γεννάω "give birth" – we run the risk of seeing the proportion of tall, good-looking, intelligent white boys increase rapidly. Independently of the societal destabilization that such a program would induce, it would weaken the species by reducing its genetic diversity.

Conversely, even though the dark history of the twentieth century has made the word *eugenics* taboo, can we, in the name of preservation of genetic diversity, refuse to allow parents to augment their children so they do not suffer from certain illnesses that could reduce their life expectancy by a few years?

It is certainly not easy to trace a clear boundary between what is ethically acceptable and what is not.

Immortality

Another issue this idea raises is the possibility of augmenting ourselves to the point of becoming immortal.

Medicine today can cure previously fatal illnesses and it *repairs* humans by replacing faulty organs with prostheses. Life expectancy is also climbing steeply. This has led some to extrapolate that we will soon live up to 120 years, a thousand years, or – why not – eternally.

Since the *Epic of Gilgamesh*, we have believed that "it is not in the nature of man to be immortal." In slowly abandoning the idea of the nature, that is, the uniqueness of man, we are led to take another look at this notion of the inevitability of death.

This reexamination takes several forms. The first is the possibility of repairing the human body. An information system is comprised more of data than of machines. We can repair the body by replacing material components, one after the other without altering the data, that is, without fundamentally modifying it. In this way, the body is rendered perennial, perhaps even eternal. This leads us to ask if we could, one day, even replace our organs, one after the other, without modifying the data that defines us as individuals.

Second, seeing various phenomena as information exchanges and algorithmic processes (see Chapter 6) provides a new view of aging, the causes of which we are beginning to understand. Are our bodies programmed to age? If this is the case, might we be able to reprogram them?

Finally, we know how to protect an information system from breaking down by backing up its data. Couldn't we, in the same way, back up all of the data that defines us as individuals on a disc as a *backup* of ourselves? Wouldn't that make us immortal?

Such speculation certainly doesn't help hospice nurses in their daily work, just as discussions of the computational capabilities of a computer that includes a black hole among its components doesn't really help computer scientists design computers that we will purchase in two years. But that is not its goal.

The goal of asking these questions is to better understand, in a scientific manner, the reasons why we are mortal, by freeing ourselves from the cultural straitjacket that insists this is our nature. Attempting to look at an old problem with fresh eyes and to free ourselves from cultural prejudices that cloud our judgment is the very essence of the scientific method.

Augmented or Diminished?

One last question behind this idea is: Does augmenting ourselves through the almost permanent connection of our brain to a computer contribute to the enrichment or, on the contrary, to the impoverishment of our minds? Some maintain, for example, that the web is destroying our ability to concentrate, that Google is making us stupid, that young people don't read anymore, and they don't write either. Even when they try, they no longer master the language enough to succeed. Are these assertions true? And are they new?

We can, for example, question the decrease in the reading ability of young people when we see that one of the greatest publishing successes of the last two decades is the Harry Potter saga, all 3,600 pages. Furthermore, this bookstore phenomenon was followed by a second phenomenon, just as interesting, the emergence of *fan fiction*, stories shared online that continue the storyline of novels, series, and *mangas*. Fan fiction writers, most often young people, are prolific writers. More than 700,000 stories continuing the Harry Potter saga have been written. This should help us put our fears about internet-connected teens who can no longer read or write in perspective.

We can also be skeptical of the novelty of these assertions. Every generation invents new words, new syntactic forms without which language would remain frozen in time, as well as new relationships with knowledge that replace the old ones and are often viewed with incomprehension by the preceding generation. For example, we know that prior to the advent of writing, history, law, and literature were transmitted orally, requiring learning long texts such as the *Iliad* or the *Odyssey* by heart from those who knew them. This tradition of memorization disappeared with the advent of writing. Five centuries after the adoption of writing by the Greeks, Plato railed against the use of writing, comparing the oral discourse of one who knows with written discourse, which is "strictly speaking, nothing but a picture."

Writing, the alphabet, printing, and now computer science have all augmented us. It is remarkable that the discourse of their detractors has remained so constant over the centuries.

18

Can an Algorithm Be Intelligent?

In the age of algorithms, new fears have arisen, including the fear that one day we will be overtaken, or even enslaved, by new beings, transhumans favored by natural selection, but also, more simply, by computers or algorithms more intelligent than us. This leads us to a question that computer scientists have been asking since the 1950s: Can an algorithm be intelligent? This question brings up two others. What does the adjective *intelligent* mean? Can we create an intelligent being?

Creating an Intelligent Being

The creation of a human being, by means other than sexual reproduction, is a recurring theme in mythology and literature. The sculptor Pygmalion, who falls in love with Galatea, the statue that he created, brought to life by Venus; Rabbi Loew, who makes a humanoid from clay, the Golem, to defend his community from pogroms; Dr. Frankenstein, whose creature escapes; Geppetto, whose wooden puppet Pinocchio suddenly comes to life; and so on.

With computer science, the question of the possibility of creating an intelligent being has left the realm of mythology, magic, and literature to become a scientific question.

A Matter of Point of View

A robot is walking in a maze, continues straight ahead, turns left, turns right, turns around, and in the end, finds the exit from the maze. We query a database: "Where can I see *2001: A Space Odyssey*?" It indicates a neighborhood cinema. It understood our question and knew how to answer it. A colleague sends us a mathematical proof and we want to verify that it's correct. No problem, many software programs can do this for us.

In these three cases, algorithms do things – find the exit to the maze, answer a question posed in natural language, verify the correctness of a mathematical proof – that, if done by human beings, requires them to use their intelligence. These algorithms seem intelligent.

However, they don't seem intelligent to everyone. After a few weeks of classes, we can have a group of students write a program to find the exit to the maze, to answer a question posed in natural language, or to verify the correctness of a mathematical proof. And if, at the end of this class, we ask these students if their programs are intelligent, they will consistently say no. As soon as they themselves have programmed them, they stop thinking that these programs possess even the slightest form of intelligence. Considering a program intelligent seems to be linked to not knowing how it works. Could intelligence be a form of opacity?

The difference between those who know how the program works and those who don't know is also illustrated by the fact that students who have programmed, for example, a robot, often try to test it in limited situations. They put it in a maze without an exit, they change the form of the maze while the robot is looking for the exit, they trip it to see if it will regain its balance. For them, this is the normal way that they test their system. For those on the outside looking in, however, this treatment may seem particularly cruel.

Intelligence and the Imitation Game

Marvin Minsky, writing in 1968, carefully avoided this problem of point of view: "Artificial intelligence is the science of making machines do things that would require intelligence if done by men."

Minksy very deftly did not say that machines themselves are intelligent. He said that, seen from the outside, they do things that would require intelligence if they were done by man.

Alan Turing said the same thing twenty years earlier when he proposed defining intelligence as the ability to pass a test. In this *Turing test*, the premises of computational thinking are apparent because Turing provides an operational and algorithmic definition of intelligence. We can also see that this definition carefully avoids making intelligence a human faculty. Whoever passes the test, perhaps an algorithm, is declared intelligent. What does the test consist of? It consists of the ability to pass as human in front of another human, that is, to be capable of imitating human intelligence.

The advantage of this definition is that it insists on the phenomenological aspect of intelligence. There is no difference between appearing intelligent and being intelligent. The disadvantage is that it is circular. In defining intelligence as the ability to imitate human intelligence, it implicitly uses the very notion it is defining.

Neither Minsky nor Turing was able to truly clarify the notion of intelligence, and we still do not have a satisfactory answer to our initial question: What is intelligence?

Intelligence or Intelligences?

Naturally, this has not prevented artificial intelligence researchers from developing algorithms that attempt to imitate one or more faculties of human intelligence: reasoning, understanding a question posed in natural language, playing chess, analyzing an image, and so on. Resolving each of these challenges requires different knowledge and techniques. Artificial intelligence is the sum of the progress achieved in these different areas.

The term *intelligence* presupposes that a sole faculty allows us to reason, understand natural language, play chess, and so on, and the term *artificial intelligence* assumes that if an algorithm were equipped with this faculty, it would be capable of completing all of these tasks equally well. However – and this is the main lesson of half a century of research in artificial intelligence – there are few points in common between language-processing algorithms and game algorithms. Just because an algorithm plays chess very well does not mean that it has other faculties that we would qualify as intelligent. An algorithm can beat the chess champion of the world and not know how to distinguish between a dog and a cat.

This observation naturally leads us to the simple idea that psychologists have been repeating for years, apparently without us hearing them: there is not only one form of intelligence.

The Concept Shredder

To say that there are several forms of intelligence, that proving a theorem is different from speaking Japanese, that playing chess is different from knowing how to orient oneself in space, is like saying that the idea of intelligence is a pseudo-concept that we should abandon and replace by other concepts, such as "ability to prove a theorem," perhaps, or "ability to speak Japanese."

What has happened to the concept of intelligence is what happened to the concepts of force, weight, or impetus when tested by science. We thought we knew what these three words meant until physicists tried to define them. They managed to define the concept of force, but their definition, "temporal derivative of momentum," would perhaps surprise those who thought they knew what this word meant. The concept of weight was divided into two concepts: weight and mass. With respect to impetus, the physicists have shown us how to do without it.

Science is a shredder of common sense concepts that, when we try to define them with precision, acquire, in the best case, a meaning that is different from their common meaning and, in general, are divided into several concepts, and sometimes simply abandoned.

The fate of the concept of intelligence will be one of those. In the best case, it will take on a meaning that is different from its general meaning, and will doubtless be divided into several concepts. Perhaps it will simply be abandoned.

The only question is why we continue to use it, including in a scientific context, for example, in the expression *artificial intelligence*. It is possible that the expectations generated by mythology and literature, Pygmalion, Loew, Frankenstein, and Geppetto go a long way in explaining our difficulty in letting go of this idea.

■ Marvin Minsky--

Marvin Minsky (1927–2016) was one of the pioneers of artificial intelligence. He also contributed to cognitive science and robotics. In his work, he sought to demonstrate that artificial intelligence was a phenomenon too complex to be captured by a single model or mechanism. Unlike electromagnetism, there was no need to look for a unifying principle; rather it would be seen as the sum of its various components. He gave us one of the rare definitions of artificial intelligence that seems to hold up to the test of time: artificial intelligence is the science of making machines do things that would require intelligence if done by man.

19

Can an Algorithm
Have Feelings?

W e used to believe that intelligence, like speech, culture, and self-awareness, made us unique. However, diluting intelligence across a variety of faculties contributes to blurring the boundary that separates man and machine. Man is better at speaking Japanese, but machines are better than man at playing chess. Perhaps one day machines will also be better at speaking Japanese. The difference between man and machine seems to be more a matter of degree than of nature, a distinction that enabled us to conceive of the idea of augmented man.

The reader may be reassured thinking that these lines were written by two human beings – as far as we know.

This blurring of boundaries gives wing to the bold and audacious, like the computer scientist and futurist Ray Kurzweil who predicts that in 2030, we will be able to back up our brain on a computer, and that in 2035, when we speak to a human, we will be speaking to a biological and non-biological hybrid intelligence. Naturally, these kinds of predictions are solely the views of their author.

However, it does appear that there are two or three little things that we perhaps do not yet share with computers: creativity, emotions, and self-awareness.

Creativity

Creativity, as it is expressed, for example, in the creation of works of art, appears to be one human faculty that is difficult to simulate. It is difficult to imagine a muse inspiring an algorithm when artists themselves tell us that the creative process follows no rules, that they do not control it, and the fact that it escapes them is precisely what characterizes their genius.

Nevertheless, without breaking with this myth of inspiration, some artists have tried to use randomness to create new works, such as the surrealists with their collaborative "exquisite corpse" pieces. Others have drawn from the combinatorial character of language to create new works, such as Raymond Queneau's *Hundred Thousand Billion Poems*. Although these two approaches are different, they have in common the idea of constructing a random or combinatorial process and then observing the sometimes unexpected result.

It is therefore not surprising that some artists at the end of the 1950s tried to use computers and algorithms to perform art. The composer Pierre Barbaud, for example, developed an automatic composition system in which randomness plays a large role. The works produced by these systems, interesting though they may be, are not yet equal to works by flesh-and-bone composers.

But who is to say that they will never be equal?

Emotions

In Spike Jonze's film *Her*, the character Theodore falls in love with his computer's operating system that he decides to name "Samantha" and to whom he gives the voice of Scarlett

Johansson. It is not surprising at all for a human being to have feelings for a computer or an algorithm. Human beings get attached every day to pets, stuffed animals, works of art, and, sometimes, to cars. Why wouldn't they get attached to computers and algorithms?

A more serious question is to know if Samantha is in love with Theodore. When he asks her the question, she answers, yes. She talks to 8,316 users, but she is in love with only 640 of them. Naturally, we could conclude that Samantha is not truly in love with Theodore because our human experience teaches us that it is not possible to be in love with so many at the same time. However, Samantha is not human.

Since the idea that a machine has feelings is disturbing, we prefer to think that Samantha is simulating feelings and emotions, but cannot really feel them. But what do the verbs *simulate* and *really feel* mean?

To shed some light on this questions, let's take a very simple example. We can program a robot so that at regular intervals it queries a temperature sensor and says, "It's cold," and turns on a radiator when the temperature goes below a certain threshold. It does not understand what it is saying any more than a myna bird, and besides, it would be very easy to reprogram it to say, "It's raining" or "It's hot," instead of "It's cold."

In any case, our nervous system functions in a fairly similar manner as a robot. When the temperature decreases, neural receptors emit a chemical signal which is then converted by other neurons into a nerve signal. This nerve signal triggers others which prompt our mouth to pronounce the words, "It's cold," and our hand to turn on the radiator. Would we say, furthermore, that we act as if we are cold, but we're not really cold? No, because if these signals cross our nervous system it is because of what we call "really being cold."

Turing's definition insisted on the phenomenological character of intelligence. In developing an idea that was already being formulated by the materialists in the eighteenth century, it underscores the absurdity of the question of knowing if an algorithm is really intelligent or if it is pretending. The same goes for the question of knowing if the robot is really cold or if it is pretending. An algorithm that behaves as if it is intelligent is intelligent. A robot that behaves as if it is cold is cold. An algorithm that behaves as if it is in love is in love.

Consciousness

The notion of consciousness, like that of intelligence, is perhaps another pseudo-concept that we'll need to replace one day with more precise ones: self-awareness, moral conscience, awareness of danger, and so on.

Such a dissolution of the notion of consciousness could lead to the idea that if we can create an artificial brain, it would be no more or no less conscious than our human brains. The question would simply no longer have meaning.

In contrast, some believe that even if we could create the perfect artificial brain, it would, like the clay Golem, be an incomplete human who would lack "the name of God": consciousness.

We leave it to the reader to choose between these two propositions.

20

Time to Choose

In the age of algorithms, inventions follow each other in rapid succession. With each invention, there are many reasons to be amazed and, also, to be worried. These inventions make possible the better world we aspire to, as well as the nightmarish world we fear.

The robots that will soon "take care of" the elderly are a good illustration of the wealth of possibilities. Their development will be considered progress if they can improve the medical care of these people, assist them in their daily lives, and increase their level of autonomy. It will be a step backward if they serve as an excuse to disengage us from one of the most human tasks there is, that of taking care of those in need.

Algorithms expand the range of possibility. They make us masters of our own destinies. But it is for us to choose. Avoiding the pitfalls of selfishness and fear will not be easy, but it is possible.

With algorithms, *Homo sapiens* has finally created a tool equal to their aspirations, a tool that makes it possible to build a world that is better, freer, and fairer. The choice is ours.